THE COMPLETE GUIDE TO OLD ENGLISH SHEEPDOGS

Malcolm Lee

Publication Data

Old English Sheepdogs
The Complete Guide to Old English Sheepdogs – First edition.
Summary: "Successfully raising an Old English Sheepdog from puppy to old age" – Provided by publisher.
ISBN: 978-1-952069-94-9
[1. Old English Sheepdogs – Non-Fiction] I. Title.

Design by Sorin Rădulescu
First paperback edition, 2020

TABLE OF CONTENTS

CHAPTER 14

CHAPTER 15

CHAPTER 1
Introducing Old English Sheepdogs

Old English Sheepdog History

Contrary to their name, Old English Sheepdogs are relative newcomers to the canine world. Their rise to fame is a noteworthy one, as the breed arguably played a small but significant part in the growth of Great Britain as an industrial powerhouse.

During the 18th century, the Industrial Revolution was in full swing. To keep the ever-expanding towns and cities fed, vast flocks of livestock were continually on the move. The arduous journey from farm to market was often dangerous, spanning tens of miles of rough countryside.

Drovers needed help, but working dogs of the time didn't fit the bill. More suited to farm work, the dogs were often too aggressive in their herding technique, resulting in some livestock reaching the markets in poor condition.

To address this problem, through selective breeding from British, European, and even Russian stock, the Old English Sheepdog evolved.

Big, tough, tireless, and brave, the steadfast loyalty and natural intelligence of the Old English Sheepdog became legendary.

Drovers in the areas of Devon and Cornwall were fond of this breed, mainly due to the dog's ability to drive livestock during the day and provide protection against highwaymen by night.

Old English Sheepdogs are broad-shouldered and stout-limbed with their natural muscularity shrouded in a blanket of shaggy fur. On the trail, their outer coat would become knotty and tangled. For this reason, the dogs were sheared right alongside the flocks they guarded.

FUN FACT

Old English Sheepdog Club of America (OESCA)

The Old English Sheepdog Club of America (OESCA) is an AKC-Member Club dedicated to preserving and protecting the Old English Sheepdog breed. OESCA maintains a referral list for Old English Sheepdog breeders and a directory for OES rescue organizations and contacts by region. The club was established in 1905. More information can be found on their website, oldenglishsheepdogclubofamerica.com

Photo Courtesy
of Stephen Gosling
Stephen Gosling Photography

Photo Courtesy of Kayla Morris

Known for their ringing bark and bear-like gait, the Old English Sheepdog adopted their trademark docked tail early on in their history. This procedure marked them as working dogs and avoided the levy of additional hunting dog and pet taxes.

This tail docking resulted in the "Bobtail" nickname, and it soon became part of the breed standard. The first Old English Sheepdog went on exhibition at the National Dog Show in England in 1865.

That inaugural event, held in Birmingham's Curzon Hall, sparked an interest in the breed on both sides of the Atlantic.

Just 13 years later saw the founding of the Old English Sheepdog Club in Great Britain. Shortly the OES Club of America was established, and the American Kennel Club officially recognized the breed.

The popularity and prestige of the Old English Sheepdog grew to such an extent in America that five of the country's wealthiest families bred and exhibited them. Legend has it that they all entered their best Bobtails in the 1904 Westminster Dog Show in New York. The result of that particular "battle royale," however, is regrettably lost in the mists of time.

One of the longest established dog shows in the world, the Westminster Dog Show, has honored the Old English Sheepdog many times. Over the years, Bobtails have proven popular with the judges, going on to win everything from "Best in Show" to multiple agility and obedience sectors.

The breed still has many die-hard fans around the world, even as far as Australia. In the mid-1800s, English farmer settlers traveled to Australia, taking the perilous three-month ocean crossing to establish the sheep industry in Western Australia. They took with them their trusty Bobtail farmhands.

Nobody knows for sure how many Old English Sheepdogs made that 13,000-mile journey. Still, you can bet your bottom dollar those seafaring Bobtails sure made the endless days at sea more bearable.

The natural herding instinct, guardianship traits, and boisterous character of those early Old English Sheepdogs live on.

These charming characteristics and traits inspired my older brother, Steven, many years ago, to adopt his first Old English Sheepdog puppy, Charlie.

Charlie's adventures and exploits are the inspiration behind this book.

Reel Dogs: The Old English Sheepdog in the Media and Film

Old English Sheepdogs were not the first dogs to star in the movies. That accolade goes to Rover the Collie, who made his debut in the 1906 black-and-white film *White Fang*.

However, over the decades, thanks to their photogenic appearance, intelligence, and clown-like behavior, Old English Sheepdogs have placed their paw prints firmly in the media.

So pull up a seat, grab some popcorn, and get ready to check out these lovable Bobtails that, through the ages, have made it onto the stage, TV, and silver screen.

1963 COCA-COLA (ADVERTISING CAMPAIGN)
The soft drink giant uses a young couple attempting to bathe an Old English Sheepdog in their 1963 advertising campaign. It complements the tag line, "Big jobs call for the Refreshing New Taste of Coca-Cola."

1961 DULUX PAINT (ADVERTISING CAMPAIGN)

The Dulux paint advertisements hit the screen in 1961. They made Old English Sheepdogs so famous in Europe that the breed became commonly referred to as "Dulux dogs."

According to Dulux, Shepton Daphnis Horsa (or Dash for short), the first of the Dulux dogs, belonged to the advertising director. During filming, Dash kept running on set to play with the actors. The footage was so comical and charming that they decided to roll with it. Dash went on to star in Dulux advertisements for the next eight years.

Over the last several decades, the paint company has featured 14 Old English Sheepdogs, 13 of which were breed champions with five Best in Show winners.

The grandly named King Hotspur of Amblegait took over the canine role from 1974–1979. Apart from innumerable public appearances on behalf of ICI/ Dulux, Amblegait guest-starred on 50+ TV shows.

A year later, in 1980, Dulux successor Gambit posed with paint as the Bobtail poster dog for Philips video recorders. By the time the shoot was a wrap, there was sufficient dog hair on set to stuff a mattress!

The company's most famous recruit, however, is Digby. Chosen from a field of 450 competitors, he went on to star in his very own Disney movie (see below).

During his illustrious media career, Digby had six stunt doubles, spent four hours a day being groomed on set, and was chauffeur-driven to the studio.

1968 CHITTY CHITTY BANG BANG (MOVIE)

In this movie, eccentric inventor Caractacus Potts, played by Dick Van Dyke, transforms an old Grand Prix car into a magical flying machine. The car then takes him and his children on an adventure-filled journey. The Potts family has a lovable, albeit clumsy, Old English Sheepdog called Edison.

1973 DIGBY, THE BIGGEST DOG IN THE WORLD (MOVIE)

Digby, an Old English Sheepdog and star of this popular adventure comedy, accidentally drinks a secret formula and grows to become 30 feet tall.

After being sold to a circus by a couple of shady characters, Digby escapes. He is pursued across the countryside by his owner Jerry (Jim Dale) and nutty professor (Spike Milligan). The professor must find him before the army does.

Digby, or Fernville Lord Digby to give him his full pedigree name, is one of the most famous Old English Sheepdogs in history. Not only did he star in *The Biggest Dog in the World,* but he also featured in the Dulux commercials during the 1970s.

1973 SERPICO (MOVIE)

Al Pacino's Oscar-winning portrayal of real-life New York cop Frank Serpico is only upstaged by his Bobtail co-star, Alfie, played by an Old English Sheepdog named Barnaby. During this crime movie, Pacino chooses Alfie from a boxful of Old English Sheepdog pups. Alfie soon becomes his lifelong and, as it turns out, only real friend. The movie is based on a true story, and even though Alfie only got to bark one line, he stole the show.

1986 LABYRINTH (MOVIE)

Labyrinth is a dark fantasy movie directed by Jim Henson. It follows Sarah, played by actress Jennifer Connelly, as she journeys through a maze to recover her baby brother from the goblin king, portrayed by David Bowie.

As the plot progresses, Sarah meets Sir Didymus, a Fox Terrier who believes himself to be a brave knight. His canine steed Ambrosius is an Old English Sheepdog. While a puppet was used in the close-up shots, a real dog was used for the full body shots.

1991 HOOK (MOVIE)

Spielberg's take on Peter Pan stars an Old English Sheepdog in the role of Nana, the Darling family's Bobtail babysitter.

While the movie also features Hollywood A-listers Dustin Hoffman, Robin Williams, and Julia Roberts, we all know who the real star of the show was.

In previous versions of Peter Pan, the starring canine role was often played by two actors in a sheepdog suit!

2001 CATS & DOGS (MOVIE)

While canines embark on a mission to create a serum to eliminate dog allergies in humans, cunning cats hatch a plot to put a stop to the project. As part of this spy comedy plot, an underground canine network exists. Its agents include Sam, an Old English Sheepdog, and Peek, a Chinese-Crested Dog.

2019 THE LITTLE MERMAID (LIVE PERFORMANCE)

The Little Mermaid, an immersive "live-to-film" concert experience, took place at the Hollywood Bowl in May 2019.

Here, the star of the show, Prince Eric's loyal dog Max, was played by a female Old English Sheepdog puppy named Bagel.

Bagel is also a therapy dog who spreads her canine love to those who need it most. Along with her co-worker Donut, she visits schools, Scout troops, and children's libraries. In 2018, she spent a few days greeting first responders and firefighters of the Woolsey Fire and comforting victims of the Borderline Shooting.

You can find out more about making this amazing breed of dogs a part of your family in the following chapters

Physical and Personality Breed Attributes

The Old English Sheepdog is a large breed with females measuring around 21" tall at the shoulder and males 22" and upward. They weigh 60-100 pounds and have a life expectancy of 10-12 years.

This robust breed of dog is surprisingly agile. Its rectangular body and stout limbs are built to take the knocks, while its shaggy coat is warm and weatherproof.

Viewing a Bobtail from the side, he should look strong and compact with sturdy limbs, but it's underneath that shaggy coat that the true picture lies.

The hips are wide and solid in appearance. They have the unusual trait of being slightly higher and broader than the shoulders.

Old English Sheepdogs' bodies appear somewhat bottom-heavy with a gentle slope down the topline (spine) toward the shoulders. This characteristic is responsible for the dogs' bear-like amble, which gives way to a graceful and surprisingly agile gait at a full run. Their feet point straight ahead and are round with well-arched toes and thick pads.

The neck is comparatively long, arched, and well-muscled. On top of this sits an impressively large head. The skull is squarely formed with plenty of room inside for that fun-loving brain!

Intelligence is immediately apparent in a Bobtail's alert and inquisitive eyes, which are generally blue, dark brown, or even one of each, and peek out from those iconic bangs.

In two distinct layers, the undercoat coat is soft and designed to keep in warmth, while the outer is coarse and weatherproof.

Colors run from varying shades of gray, blue merle, blue, or grizzle with the head being mainly white with splashes of shading on the ears, eyes, or both.

Darker shading usually falls along the back and hindquarters rather like a draped blanket. Regardless of the color combination, coats need regular and prolonged brushing and grooming to prevent tangling and knotting.

Contrary to popular belief, OESs can't see out through their dense hair, so when it's not cut short, it's important to tie it out of the way.

Personality Attributes

Despite their gentle looks and clownish antics, Bobtails are intelligent and bright. At first sight, this breed of dog is affable and charming, but beneath the shaggy coat lies a strong-willed, free, and independent thinker.

A good-natured breed, Old English Sheepdogs can develop an inseparable bond with their owners. While they are courageous, territorial, and excellent watchdogs, they aren't guard dogs. However, they take their responsibility for their human family seriously.

Sometimes too seriously, like my nephew, Ben, discovered with Charlie. Like all teenagers, Ben was busy listening to music while walking to school. He didn't notice Charlie happily lolloping along, following in his footsteps. Charlie had taken advantage of Ben's forgetfulness, nudging open the unlocked yard gate with his sizeable nose. It wasn't until Charlie caught up with Ben at a crosswalk that he realized his canine companion had been loyally watching his back the whole time!

For families with very young children, a Bobtail's bumbling gait and boisterousness around the house is something to take into account when choosing this breed of dog.

Bobtails are the ideal breed for families with older children, as an attention-seeking Old English Sheepdog relishes interaction with his family. This agile dog loves to explore and enjoys nothing more than a good romp, making him an ideal companion for energetic teens.

Due to their herding heritage, Bobtails need daily exercise to disperse all that energy. However, this isn't an excuse to leave your dog alone in the yard for long periods. Being a yard dog is not ideal for any breed, but it's particularly detrimental to an OES who thrives on human interaction. Worse still, it can lead to unwanted or even aggressive behavior. When you're inside your home, your dog should be as well, especially in hot or humid weather, when his double-layered coat can become uncomfortable.

Old English Sheepdogs are sociable and readily accept visitors into their home. As for mixing with other household pets, Bobtails are not known as cat botherers and tend to be generous and tolerant of other family dogs. It's essential, though, that socializing takes place from a young age.

Old English Sheepdogs are sweet-tempered and love to be the center of attention. They will let you know when they feel you're not taking enough notice of them. They will do this either vocally with their trademark ringing bark or by treating you to a free face wash. Bobtail tongues aren't generally bigger than those of other large breeds, but they do have permanently wet beards, which add to the face-licking fun.

Is This the Breed for You?

"OES are very intelligent dogs and need an owner that is not afraid of being the pack leader. They are great family dogs and love to be right next to their people."

DEA FREIHEIT
SnowDowne Old English Sheepdogs

Photo Courtesy of Linda Gallagher

Large dogs find themselves abandoned in rescue centers, on the streets, and in dog pounds for many reasons. These can include bad behavior brought about by a lack of training. Still, more often than not, it's as a direct result of breed ignorance.

When considering taking on a large breed, or any size dog for that matter, prospective owners need to do some thorough research.

Dog ownership is a serious commitment, so before you fall head over heels for this affable clown, make sure you're aware of all the accompanying baggage; the good and the bad!

Lifestyle Needs

An Old English Sheepdog doesn't care if you are a doctor or a DJ. What he is interested in, though, is the level of interaction he can expect from his new owner and family.

Bobtails are one of the most sociable breeds in the dog universe, and rigidly built into their DNA is the desire for human company.

The amount of interaction you can give your dog will have a direct impact on his mental health. This breed of dog is particularly susceptible to loneliness, and long periods of regular isolation may see him become possessive and, in some cases, adversely affect his personality.

These athletic dogs are headstrong, and without correct and ongoing socialization, they will test their boundaries. They may also become disruptive and unruly in the home.

So ask yourself, can you commit to a large dog that is, at times, needy?

Physical Space Needs

Bobtails are one of the best freestyle sleepers you'll ever come across. That is to say, your dog will pick a spot and call it his own. He may get cozy on your bed, curl up on the sofa, or lie across a high foot-traffic area. As long as he likes the spot, he'll just park, collapse, and check out.

The physical size of the floor space in your home is not a significant issue for an Old English Sheepdog. As long as he has enough room to move around comfortably, he'll be happy.

This breed of dog is not best suited to living in a small space or apartment. As they grow, Bobtails' natural stature gives them a rear end–heavy posture, which translates to a natural sway when they walk. Add to this a lolloping gait and long bangs, and you have a large dog bumping into furniture, precious belongings, and small children.

Exercise Needs

Although they enjoy lazing around, Old English Sheepdogs are not couch potatoes. They need daily exercise, regular walks, and ideally playtime sessions.

Purpose-bred for covering miles of rough countryside every day, daily exercise is non-negotiable for these dogs. They need sufficient outdoor space to explore.

Surprisingly agile for their size, OESs love to run, jump, and fetch. Your Bobtail will have stacks of energy, and to become a well-rounded, friendly, and happy dog, he will need to blow off quite a lot of steam.

Grooming Needs

The three rules of Bobtail ownership are brush, brush, and brush once more! Old English Sheepdogs shed a lot and their fluffy coat needs a great deal of upkeep.

You will need to set aside at least 30 minutes per day for basic grooming. Brushing will result in enough fluff to stuff a pillowcase. Bathing is recommended every 8-10 weeks but will depend on how dirty your dog gets in the meantime.

Photo Courtesy of Cathy Hausman

Bobtails aren't fazed by mud or bad weather, making post-walk clean-ups a given, which is a significant consideration for anyone who is particularly house-proud. They also drool a lot, and their shaggy coats attract dirt and debris, which can end up on your floor coverings and soft furnishings.

Training Needs

Bobtails are big, bumbling, and boisterous, all good reasons why training is essential. You will need to commit to training and set aside time for obedience lessons from eight weeks onward.

Their headstrong nature is also why socializing is important, too, and should be a major part of your training program.

Have a Family Meeting

Before you make your final decision as to whether or not an OES is for you, it's a good idea to have a chat with the rest of the family and make sure they can commit to his needs and care.

These are just some of the topics you could discuss:

- Who is going to be the dog's primary caregiver?
- Who will take responsibility for feeding, making sure he has enough water, exercise, and grooming?
- If you have children in your household, you could give them responsibilities for different aspects of your dog's care. While older children can help exercise or groom a family pet, younger kids can keep toys tidy or help with cleaning and filling water bowls.
- Set limits. Is your Bobtail going to be allowed to sit on the sofa, sleep on your bed, etc.?
- Are any rooms in the house off limits?

If you can cater 100 percent to all a Bobtail's needs, then yes, this breed is the one for you.

Breed-Specific Health Problems

The majority of Old English Sheepdogs live a happy and healthy life, enjoying a lifespan of some 10-12 years. However, they are susceptible to a number of health issues and conditions, some of which are hereditary. These are something that you should discuss with your breeder and veterinarian.

Here are some of the most common breed-specific issues and conditions:

- **Cancer:** This disease is the number one cause of death among Old English Sheepdogs. The three most common forms of cancer in Bobtails are Osteosarcoma (malignant bone tumors), Lymphoma (cancer of the lymphatic system), and Hemangiosarcoma (cancer of the blood vessels).

- **Canine Hip Dysplasia:** The size and weight of an Old English Sheepdog results in stress on the skeletal structure. As a result, your dog's hips and elbows are at risk of this inherited disease that causes the joints not to develop correctly. It results in stiffness and arthritis, which can become a problem as the dog gets older.

- **Cataracts:** This deformation of the lens of the eye can lead to poor vision or blindness. Although more common in older dogs, it can develop early on, or even be present in dogs at birth.

Photo Courtesy of Julian Gallina

- **Cerebellar Abiotrophy:** This condition, although not painful, causes a progressive loss of muscular coordination; however, it doesn't cause muscular weakness or affect the dog's mind.

- **Deafness:** Bobtails are susceptible to deafness, either complete or partial, in one or both ears.

- **Ear and Eye Infections:** Dogs with large or hairy ears like Old English Sheepdogs are more prone to infections than some other breeds. Unkempt and long hair over your dog's eyes can lead to conjunctivitis and other eye infections.

- **Gastric Torsion or Bloat:** This condition is present in dogs with narrow, deep chests, which puts the Old English Sheepdog at more risk than some other breeds. When bloat occurs, the stomach twists in on itself and fills with gas. This twisting action results in the blood supply to the stomach and sometimes the spleen being cut off.

- **Hypothyroidism:** Like many other large breeds, Old English Sheepdogs can suffer from a congenital conditional called hypothyroidism. This condition results from a lower production of thyroid gland hormones. Symptoms of this include unexplained weight gain, lethargy, reoccurring skin infections, and excessive shedding.

- **Obesity:** Old English Sheepdogs need a lot of exercise. Without enough physical exertion to burn off the calories, your Bobtail can pile on the pounds. Excess weight has the potential to cause joint problems as well as unduly straining the heart, lungs, kidneys, and liver. Your dog could also develop breathing problems and suffer from high blood pressure.

TOP TIP

Due to the shaggy coat, it's easy to miss extra pounds, so check your Bobtail's weight at regular intervals.

- **Progressive Retinal Atrophy:** A common eye disease in OESs, progressive retinal atrophy (PRA) is a disorder of the retina. Although not painful, it can occur in both eyes, which can appear dilated, or the pupils may be glassy.

This list may appear daunting but well-bred and correctly cared-for Old English Sheepdogs are a resilient breed. They can take the knocks and overcome the majority of health problems.

As is always the case, the moment you detect or suspect a potential health problem, consult your veterinarian sooner rather than later. A lot of health conditions are entirely treatable or easily manageable when detected early.

Photo Courtesy
of Lorraine Paoletti

Expenses: The Bottom Line

While Old English Sheepdogs are not the most expensive breed in the world, there are initial and ongoing costs to Bobtail ownership.

If you are looking to buy from a breeder, you will want to buy the best OES puppy you can find. Remember, though, professional dog breeding is a costly and time-consuming process.

This fact is reflected in the price asked by reliable breeders. Prices can range from $1,200-1,500 depending on the dog's bloodline.

The cost of this initial purchase is dramatically reduced for rescue Old English Sheepdogs from a reputable and recognized rescue center. Most centers re-home dogs fully vaccinated and either neutered or spayed.

Costs will vary, and a not-for-profit organization may ask you for a donation, which could set you back $300-600 depending on the age of the dog.

Depending on the state or county, you could need a license, and there may also be a charge for registering your dog.

Setting the initial outlay for your Bobtail aside for a moment, be aware that buying a large dog is an ongoing financial commitment.

Health and Veterinarian Costs

Puppies and vaccinations are par for the course. Unvaccinated dogs should not be allowed off your property for walks in public places until they've had all their necessary immunizations. You can, if you want, carry your puppy and introduce him to the outside world that way until he receives his vaccines.

The primary immunization is a combination vaccine commonly known as a 5-1 shot. This vaccine protects against canine distemper virus, two types of adenovirus, parainfluenza, and parvovirus. There is no known cure to these diseases, which is why vaccination is so important.

Annual boosters are also recommended, along with general and regular health checks. You will also need to talk to your vet about worming and flea treatments and costs.

If it's not your intention to breed from your Bobtail, it is wise to get him or her neutered (male) or spayed (female). Doing this will also lessen the chance of either gender developing some forms of cancers later on in life. This topic will be expanded on in a later chapter.

At some time in your dog's life, he will likely have some form of an acci-dent-related injury. He may also, during his 10-12 year lifespan, succumb to a canine illness or need emergency dental work. For these reasons, it's a sensible idea to get pet insurance. Ask your vet for recommendations.

Photo Courtesy
of Diane Nielsen

Equipment Costs

These costs tend to be one-offs, but Bobtails don't stay cute bundles of fluff for long, so some items may need replacing due to size or wear and tear.

These may include:

- A crate (opt for one large enough for an adult-size dog)
- Sleeping mat or dog bed
- Bedding
- Collar, lead, harness, and ID tags
- Food and water bowls
- Dog-friendly snacks
- Toys and puzzles
- Grooming and bathing equipment (brushes, nail clippers, eye and ear cleaning wipes, toothbrushes, shampoo, and conditioner)

Food Costs

Old English Sheepdogs need good quality food and the best people to advise on the type, brand, and quantity is the breeder. Alternatively, talk with your vet or check out an owner's club or society for recommendations.

Specific food costs will depend entirely on the quality, brand, and supplier you decide to go with. Keep in mind an average adult OES Bobtail will consume approximately 500 grams (17.6-ounces) of dry food per day. You will, therefore, be purchasing around 15 kilograms (33 pounds) of food every month for your dog's 10-12 year life span.

So, while we can't offer a precise food cost estimate, it is safe to say that feeding an Old English Sheepdog is a much larger investment than feeding a Chihuahua!

To conclude, here is the bottom line:

- The initial cost of a puppy – $1200-1500
- The initial cost of Bobtail rescue – $300-600 (no added vaccinations or neutering/spaying fees)
- Vet (vaccinations, flea and worm treatments, micro-chipping) – $100-300
- Neutering – $100-150 (depending on weight)
- Spaying – $200-300 (depending on weight)
- Equipment – $150-200
- Food costs are dependent on brand, quality, etc.

You may also want to take into consideration other expenses such as kenneling, dog walking, private grooming, or specialized training. Costs for this will depend entirely on your specific needs and location.

Suffice to say, owning an Old English Sheepdog is a considerable commitment; emotionally, physically, and practically – so do the math and embark upon this incredible journey armed with all the facts.

CHAPTER 2
Spoiled for Choice

Puppy versus Adult Rescue

H aving made that all-important decision to welcome an Old English Sheepdog into your home, the next question to ask yourself is, should you opt for a puppy or an adult?

As a dog owner, I have purchased puppies from breeders and also adopted adult rescues. Pups and adults bring with them their unique joys and challenges. Let's explore both avenues to help you make the right decision for you, your family, and your circumstances.

Photo Courtesy of Ashley Calhoun

Puppy

Let's face it, all puppies are adorable, but this is especially the case with Old English Sheepdogs. The excitement and suspense of waiting weeks to collect your tiny Bobtail is like nothing else.

Puppies are a blank slate. In positive terms, this means they're unlikely to have any pre-existing behavioral issues, and you will be their first and only family. Therefore, the bond you form together will be both special and strong.

My brother Steven bought his OES Charlie as a puppy for this very reason. Puppies are generally very tolerant and non-aggressive, making safer playmates for small children. With a young son, Ben, in the house, this was an important factor. It also gave Ben and Charlie time to bond and get used to one another, before Charlie grew into a large and boisterous brother!

The negative side of this is that a blank slate needs teaching – and lots of it! In the same way you would raise a human baby, you will need to guide and train your puppy in all areas, from going to the bathroom, sleeping through the night, and using good behavior.

While your adorable new family member will arrive small and manageable, he will soon grow to be a 60 to 100-pound bundle of muscular energy. This enthusiasm and vigor needs directing from a young age. If you don't invest time in the early days and begin training your OES puppy, you could have an unruly adult on your hands.

Old English Sheepdogs are loyal and loving; they live to please their human family. Being continually reprimanded for bad behavior can lead to your dog feeling depressed and further acting out.

To harness the strong-willed and intelligent nature of your Bobtail constructively, you must establish routines, address unwanted behavior, and begin training from the outset. This commitment can mean taking substantial time off from work to stay home with your new puppy during their first few weeks. If this isn't practicable, you should consider the services of a pet sitter, friend, or extended family member to help out.

Conclusion

Purchasing a puppy offers a unique opportunity for your family to form a strong bond with your new arrival from the outset. You will receive a blank slate, allowing you to shape your puppy's personality.

On the flip side, you must have the time, energy, and willingness to guide them through their early developmental stages. Be prepared for sleepless nights while your puppy settles into a sleep routine and requires regular trips to the bathroom.

Adult Rescue

Adult OESs may find their way to a rescue center for several different reasons; most often, it's for one that's not their fault. For example, their previous owners may be unwell or unable to care for them due to a change in financial circumstances.

Photo Courtesy of Michelle Villalobos

For a breed that is loyal and family-oriented, this separation can be very traumatic and potentially result in negative behavior or trust issues.

However, a dog's capacity for love is infinite. Although you may not be his first family, there is something incredibly special about being his last, especially if your dog's previous owners didn't express a lot of love and kindness. It may take more patience to bond with an adult rescue dog than a puppy, but your connection will be just as strong, if not more.

A common misconception is that adopting an adult dog means he will already be house-trained. The reality is, your adopted dog's previous family may have been neglectful and failed to train him adequately. You and your family may need to start potty and sleep training from scratch.

Alternatively, an adult rescue dog may have received some form of training. However, it will still take patience and guidance to help him refresh those skills and apply them to meet your own expectations.

One of the challenges with rescue pets is that often the

center will not have a complete picture of a dog's background and history. They will likely be unable to tell you about potential genetic illnesses or give you a full picture of any health issues. Bear in mind, some dogs may have had traumatic experiences in their past that the center is unaware of.

You will need to tread carefully and thoughtfully, keeping an eye open for any "triggers" that seem to elicit an aggressive or fearful response in the dog. These triggers can offer a clue to bad experiences the dog may have had. For example, if he cowers to avoid being put in a dog crate, he may have been locked up for long periods by his previous owners. If he becomes distraught when you leave him alone, your Bobtail may have separation issues.

There is also the possibility that an adopted Bobtail could have food-guarding issues. These are not uncommon in dogs that have experienced life in a rescue center.

The good news is, not all rescue center dogs will have challenging pasts. The unique thing about adopting an adult is that you can see the fully grown size and personality before bringing a dog home. Old English Sheepdogs can reach up to 100 pounds. Seeing them at their adult weight and height can help you confirm that you're able to cope with such a large dog.

A puppy may be a blank slate, but an adult dog will have a unique character. You will be able to meet him and find the best fit for you and your family. Although, you will often find that a rescue dog chooses you, not the other way around!

Conclusion

Giving a rescue dog a second chance at happiness is incredibly rewarding, but also challenging. The dog's previous family background and health history may be unknown. You may have to begin from scratch with housetraining or at least help the dog to remember what he has learned previously.

Gaining a Bobtail's trust through patience and kindness can result in an extraordinary and unbreakable bond.

The Choice Is Yours

Bringing an Old English Sheepdog into your home will require lots of patience and commitment, whether he is a young puppy or a fully grown adult. Regardless of the decision you make, one thing is for sure; you have the guarantee of a best friend for life.

Photo Courtesy
of Kristi Callanan

Choosing a Breeder and Breeder Expectations

The majority of would-be Old English Sheepdog owners will no doubt go the puppy route. In which case, being a purebred dog, it makes sense to seek out an OES-specific breeder.

Remember, a Bobtail's life expectancy is approximately 10-12 years. So your choice of puppy will have a huge impact on your family. This fact alone makes due diligence a must.

How to Find the Right Bobtail Breeder for You

So how do you start your search for a breeder? First, check out the Old English Sheepdog Club of America (OESCA). The club dedicates itself to responsible Bobtail ownership and preserves and protects the breed.

OESCA has an ethical code for breeders to follow. While the club doesn't endorse specific breeders, and not all members are included in the list, it's an excellent place to start your search. Here, you will find a list of OES breeders organized by state with names, contact numbers, and, in most cases, email addresses.

You can also surf the internet for any OESCA clubs in your local area. Firsthand advice and knowledge from current Bobtail owners is invaluable and can give you a real insight into Old English Sheepdog ownership.

Finally, talk to your local veterinarian. He may be aware of up and coming litters or be able to put you in touch with current owners along with any reputable breeders known to the clinic.

Breeder research is not something that you can hurry. You are about to make a life-changing decision.

Below are some useful tips to help you choose the right breeder for you:

- If the breeder has a website, scrutinize all the images on the site. Ask yourself; do the premises, kennels, and facilities look well cared for?

- Are there photographs of past and present sires and dams?

- Can you visit the breeder in person? If a breeder says no to this request, then cross them off your list.

- When visiting a breeder, check out how any existing dogs on the premises react to you, the breeder, and members of staff. Happy dogs are more likely to be healthy, well-adjusted dogs.

- If there is a litter to see, great! If not, can you see the sire or dam? Ask how many litters the dam has produced, and the date of the last one. If either dog isn't present, don't be afraid to ask why.

- Is the breeder able to give you any testimonials from previous owners? Are you able to touch base with them for a chat? This information is useful for finding out about the temperament and health of the breeder's litters, along with any positive or negative breeder experiences.

Photo Courtesy
of Bonnie Goldsmith

- Ask lots of questions and eliminate any potential breeders that are evasive. Breeders should be caring, open to giving advice and information, and knowledgeable about the Old English Sheepdog breed.
- Be wary of breeders with multiple dog breeds for sale. It may be a warning sign that they are more interested in profit than a quality "product."
- Ask what happens to any dogs that become too old to breed. Some breeders euthanize their dogs that can no longer reproduce, and the answer to this question will give you a good insight into the breeder's integrity.

Remember, both you and the breeder have a responsibility to the puppy. So a potential breeder may also question you to make sure that you are a good fit and suitable to adopt one of his litter. Don't be offended if this happens. It's a good sign!

Most puppies are sold as pets, meaning their temperament and social skills are key. However, if you intend to show your OES, some breeders specialize in producing litters from certified breed champions. These will favor breed standards over social skills. You can search for these on the internet or even seek out Old English Sheepdog shows to attend.

Once you are happy with your choice of a breeder, you can delve a little deeper with more specific questions that relate directly to purchasing a puppy. These could include:

- How long has your chosen breeder been breeding Old English Sheepdogs?
- Do dogs and puppies live outside or inside? This question can help give you an idea on your puppy's socialization experience.
- Is it possible to meet the puppy's parents?
- Have the sire and dam had any health tests, and is there proof they have no breed-specific genetic diseases?
- Will your chosen puppy have a record of up-to-date immunizations?
- Does the puppy come with a guarantee?
- Is there a puppy-care pack with advice on how to care for your new puppy?
- In the event of something going wrong, is there a return policy or rehoming policy in place?
- Do you offer ongoing support during the lifetime of a Bobtail?
- At what age can you take a puppy home? If the breeder allows the puppy to leave before it reaches eight weeks old, this is a major red flag. In some states, it is a legal requirement that a puppy stays with its mother for at least eight weeks. Even if not illegal, be aware that it's during this time a puppy learns the type of life lessons only another dog can teach. These include bite-inhibition and pack hierarchy.

What Should You Expect from the Breeder Once You Have Bought Your Puppy?

Once you have chosen your puppy, both parties (you and the breeder) will need to sign an agreement or contract.

This document will differ from breeder to breeder. Some may be simple, while others are more in-depth.

They should, however, include the breeder's terms, the adopter's responsibility, and any relevant health guarantees.

Read through the documentation carefully and make sure you are happy to comply with its terms. It should consist of the following information:

Documentation

The documentation that comes with a registered pup generally includes its pedigree. This paperwork will have details of your puppy's parents, grandparents, and great-grandparents.

Registration documents come in two versions; Limited and Full. The former means that any litters from the named dog cannot be registered and cannot compete in conformation dog shows, only skill-related shows.

The latter type of registration means your dog may produce litters, and you can register him as long as both parents are also registered and the same breed.

It is important to note that being registered is not a guarantee of health or temperament. True lineage and proof of a purebred is only guaranteed by an accompanying DNA certificate, which some breeders may also offer.

Guarantee

Most reputable Bobtail breeders provide a guarantee as part of the sale. If this is the case, you need to read it carefully and check out the small print before you sign anything or pay a deposit.

Photo Courtesy of Jennifer Schaefer

Guarantees generally relate to genetic defects, but you need to pay good attention to the wording. The guarantee may, for example, state that it covers "life-threatening defects."

On the surface, this sounds good. However, it cleverly skates around non-life-threatening issues such as deafness, hip dysplasia, and blindness, which can be genetically inherited due to poor breeding.

Check to what age the guarantee covers along with any paragraphs relating to refunds for unhealthy pups. There may also be a section on what happens in the event of you needing to re-home your dog.

Health Check Paperwork

As you know now, a registration and pedigree certificate is no guarantee of health. It is advisable to ask what health checks the parents and or puppy have had. These can include hip X-rays and sight and hearing tests.

Invested breeders may well have an Orthopedic Foundation for Animals (OFA) rating. The Foundation has a dog-specific health program called the Canine Health Information Center (CHIC). It also collects health information, offers certified tests for breed-specific diseases, and registers the information in an accessible database.

What to Look for in a Puppy

"Temperament is #1 on my list. A proper personality is a dog that knows no stranger and yet is very loyal to its owner."

DEA FREIHEIT
SnowDowne Old English Sheepdogs

After much consideration, you have decided to take the plunge and purchase an Old English Sheepdog puppy. You have carried out your research and selected a breeder. Now for the exciting part; choosing your puppy!

Although this is a fun time, don't let enthusiasm cloud your judgment. This new addition will be a part of your family for the next 10-12 years. Therefore, selecting the best puppy to fit your family and your lifestyle is an important task, and one to take seriously.

Here, we will run through some important tests and things to look out for. It's easy to be distracted by an adorable litter of Bobtail puppies, but make sure to get back on track. Jot down notes or take this whole list with you; a reputable breeder will not be offended as it merely confirms your commitment to being a responsible dog owner.

Puppy Personalities

Although each puppy will have its own unique character, it's possible to group them into several main personality types. Understanding these personality types and identifying which is the best fit for your family will give you a clear idea of precisely what to look for when visiting the litter.

Personality Type	Family Fit
Bully: A 'bully' pup may initially appear interactive and social, but after closer inspection will play rough, often stealing toys from other puppies. He may be trying to seek higher ground. He will do this either by scaling the sides of the enclosure or climbing on the backs of his littermates.	Although the name may sound negative, 'bully' pups are often resilient, confident, and smart. They can adapt well to new situations. However, harnessing these personality traits requires an ability to identify when such behaviors cross the line and immediately challenge said behavior. 'Bully' pups are better suited to single people or couples as they respond best to continual and consistent direction.
Rebel: A fun-loving and quick-thinking puppy. He will likely be full of energy, engaged, and lead play with his littermates but less aggressively than a 'bully.' 'Rebel' pups are often a little cheeky. Look out for him nibbling your fingers or clothes, or the ears of his siblings.	'Rebel' pups are personable and playful, but not overly headstrong. They tend to be a little naughty, so need any destructive behavior to be nipped in the bud. With heaps of enthusiasm and a sense of adventure, they are a good fit for an active owner or family with teenage children.
Eager to Please: Perhaps the easiest to identify, an 'eager to please' puppy will run straight to you, often nuzzling your hand to resume petting if you stop. He will be enthusiastic and enjoy being held and played with.	'Eager to please' pups are full of love and affection. Their training will need to be consistent and revolve heavily around positive, rather than negative, reinforcement. Thanks to their love of play and touch, they are ideal for families with younger kids or first-time dog owners.
Independent Thinker: Although this type of puppy is happy to play and interact with his siblings in short bursts, you will likely see him move away and sit separately from the main group. He will chew a toy alone.	'Independent thinkers' are intelligent, sensitive, and quick to learn. They do best in stable and calm home environments with older couples or families with grown children.

Laid Back: A 'laid back' puppy will often play for a short time before you see him lie down and take a nap. He will engage in play with his littermates but will often concede in competitive games, such as tug of war.

'Laid back' pups tend to be less intelligent than other personality types, so it will require more repetition when it comes to training. However, their balanced approach to sleep and play makes them well-rounded and manageable. Thanks to their non-competitive and non-aggressive demeanor, they are suitable companions for very young children too.

Timid: It is easy to spot the 'timid' pup in a litter. He will be shy and reserved. He may approach you by crawling on his belly or with his back arched in submission once his siblings have run away from you. He will be sweet and gentle.

It can take a lot of time and patience to help build a 'timid' pup's self-esteem and confidence. They do best with single owners or child-free couples with prior experience who can devote a lot of time to one-on-one bonding and training. 'Timid' pups make very loyal and close companions to their owners but are not ideal for those who like to continually host visitors in their homes.

Be realistic when deciding what type of puppy you want to offer a home to. While you may like the idea of helping a timid pup come out of his shell or training a bully pup to reach his potential, be realistic about your experience and capabilities.

As a general rule of thumb, first-time dog owners do best when paired with an eager-to-please personality type.

Chat with the breeder; they will have spent a lot of time with the puppies and may already have identified the different personality types within the litter. As such, good breeders can help you select the dog that is right for you.

Before the Visit

First, check with your selected breeder how many litters the mother (bitch) has had. Ideally, the mother will have had at least two previous litters by the same father (stud). This fact is significant as it ensures the coupling has a history of producing healthy puppies.

Ask your chosen breeder to notify you as soon as the litter is born. Arrange to visit as quickly as possible; often, the best puppies from a litter are reserved very early on. Although the breeder will likely not permit you to meet the puppies until they are at least 6-7 weeks old, you can aim to ensure you are at the top of the waiting list.

Photo Courtesy of Dana Baumgartnern

Once you have set up a meeting, decide who you will take along. It is best to avoid involving young children at this early stage. A child will most likely take a shine to the cutest or most playful puppy in a litter, not necessarily the one with the most suitable temperament. Once a child has bonded with a puppy, it can be near impossible to change their mind, so it is best to leave children out of the initial selection process!

If possible, try and take a knowledgeable friend or family member along with you who is experienced with puppies in general and/or specifically with Old English Sheepdogs.

Before leaving for your visit, gather a few items;
- A copy of this list
- A ball or toy with a squeaker
- A small flashlight (or you can use your phone's light)

During the Visit

First, narrow down your options. Jumping in and interacting with the whole litter can be overwhelming and distract you from the task in hand. Identify any puppies with your preferred personality type, either through observation or with help from the breeder.

Once you have a smaller selection, interact with the puppies, one by one, while carrying out your character and physical checks.

Character Checks

Pick each puppy up and gently hug him to you. It is usual for him to wriggle a little, but a slowness to settle, squealing, or showing distress is not a good sign.

Set the puppy back down and move back a little, crouching down or sitting. Call the puppy to you by patting the ground, clicking your fingers, or quietly whistling. A puppy that comes to you quickly likely feels comfortable in your presence and shows an affinity with humans.

Next, gently touch the puppy's ears, paws, and tail. A good breeder will have handled the puppies from a young age, and as such, they should be comfortable with human contact.

Take the ball or toy that you have brought with you and try to engage the puppy in play or get his attention. Depending on your chosen personality type, you may not be looking for a puppy who relishes energetic, sustained play. However, the puppy should still at least acknowledge the toy and display a passing interest. Lethargy or disinterest could be potential signs of illness.

Very importantly, test the puppy's level of jaw control. Allow the puppy to mouth your fingers and hands. As he becomes more forceful, respond with an immediate, high-pitched "ouch," and watch carefully for his reaction. An appropriate response is for the puppy to react to your pain immediately, either ceasing or reducing the level of force with which he is biting. He will likely continue after a short pause, but this is not a bad sign—he's just a puppy, after all. However, puppies must show early signs of jaw control for them to grow to be non-aggressive adults.

Photo Courtesy
of Anya N. Tirelli

Physical Checks

Give the whole litter, not just your shortlisted options, a once-over. They should be neither skinny nor fat, but round with a shiny coat.

Take an in-depth look at each puppy's mouth, nose, ears, eyes, and rear end. If the enclosure is dark or has low lighting, use the flashlight or phone light you brought along to make sure you don't miss anything.

Begin with the mouth; the jaw should be neither undershot nor over-shot. The gums should be pink, and the teeth clean. The nose should have no crust or discharge around the nostrils. Ears should be clean. Eyes must be clear, alert, and bright. There should be no signs of inflammation or discharge around the rear end or genitalia.

Run some preliminary hearing and vision tests using your squeaky ball or toy. Squeak the ball or toy close to each puppy to check that he reacts to the noise. Afterward, while the puppy is sitting or standing, roll the ball or throw the toy in front of them, to ensure they register the moving object.

Observe the puppy's breathing; he should not be continually coughing or sneezing. Breaths should be steady and quiet.

Finally, watch how the puppy walks and runs. The puppy's gait should show no signs of limping or stiffness, which can be early signs of joint and bone issues.

Things to Remember

- Preparation is key. Sit down with your family and decide on precisely what type of puppy you want to welcome into your home.
- Choose with your head, not your heart. Keep referring back to your notes to remind yourself what you are looking for.
- Ask the breeder for their opinions and observations of the puppies in the litter, but don't allow yourself to be pushed toward a specific puppy if he doesn't match your criteria.
- Take your time and complete all your checks. A good breeder will understand that it is an important decision and will not rush you.
- If none of the puppies suit your family, don't be afraid to walk away. Your Old English Sheepdog will be with you for 10-12 years. Although it may be disappointing not to immediately find the puppy you want, it is preferable to making the wrong decision.

Rescue Research and What to Look For

In a canine utopia, all Old English Sheepdog puppies would remain in loving forever homes until they cross over the rainbow bridge. Sadly, in reality, this is not the case.

There are various reasons why a dog becomes homeless. Some dogs may be abandoned or neglected, while others are abused.

There are a number of homeless OESs looking for new families. The object of a good rescue center or shelter is to bring these unfortunate dogs together with loving people looking to adopt.

Once you have decided to offer a home to a rescue Bobtail, the next thing to do is begin the search for a suitable rescue center. As with most things in the 21st century, the best place to start is the internet.

A web search for Old English Sheepdog rescue centers will give you plenty of hits for breed-specific rescues and shelters throughout the country.

Some centers may be in far-off states, so first, decide how far you are prepared to travel. Do this before you check out the photo gallery of available Bobtails for adoption. It's heartbreaking to fall for a particular dog only to discover it's at the opposite end of the country.

Search an OES rescue center's website for:

- Details of its history
- Terms and Conditions of adoption
- Testimonials from previous adopters
- Links to a Facebook page or blog

- A photo gallery of Old English Sheepdogs available for adoption
- Vaccination, neutering, spaying, and health check documentation
- Microchip details
- Adoption fees

At least 25 percent of dogs in a canine shelter are purebred, so contact local shelters and animal control to see if any abandoned OESs are looking for homes.

It is also worth checking with your veterinarian and sending out emails to organizers of any local dog training and obedience classes. Either of these may have local information about an abandoned Bobtail or, failing that, helpful advice.

When you do find a suitable rescue center, reach out and check if you need to make an appointment. If so, arrange a time and date to visit. If this isn't possible, talk to the rescue center on the telephone or email them with any questions or specific concerns.

Let them know you're serious about adopting and be prepared to answer plenty of questions. A good rescue center will want to feel assured that the homeless dog is going to a good, caring home. Don't be surprised if they ask for a home visit too. They need to make sure any prospective adopter not only meets their requirements but is also a good fit with the chosen dog.

Shelters today are careful to make sure that adoptions run smoothly, so they will each have their unique adoption application process. Many will carry out follow-up checks, too, to make sure everything is going well. This service can be useful in helping you overcome any teething problems with your new companion.

The rescue center may or may not have specific information on a particular Bobtail in their care. Regardless of this, the dog will have been evaluated upon arrival at the center. His temperament will have been assessed, as well as how he interacts with people and other animals.

It is a good idea to chat with the staff or volunteers at the shelter. They may have valuable inv sight into a particular dog's personality, along with information on how he interacts with other dogs and people.

A good rescue center will pass on all relevant details, including any potential problems to look out for, so ask about any known past or ongoing health issues.

The center should also offer ongoing help and advice, make sure vaccinations are up to date, and that dogs for re-homing are spayed or neutered.

Once you have found the Old English Sheepdog you feel is a good fit, the next stage is to spend a little time getting to know him. This step is important, so don't try and hurry the process. An abandoned dog may take a little time to trust you. An excellent way to earn his trust is by taking him for a short walk.

Doing this removes him from the stressful kennel environment. It will give you a better indication of his behavior and reveal if he has undergone any basic training.

Don't be put off if a Bobtail is either scared or over-enthusiastic at the prospect of leaving the confines of the shelter. His exercise opportunities will have been minimal, so he could be excited to explore or scared to leave the safety of his kennel. Again, be patient before judging his behavior.

Ask the kennel worker if you can offer the dog a treat. If the dog is curious but non-aggressive, it's a good sign. If the dog growls, it could be an indication of food-related issues.

Choosing to adopt an adult Old English Sheepdog rescue gives a dog a second chance at life. Not only that, but it also makes room for the center to rescue another abandoned, neglected, or abused animal.

Canine Conundrum: The Gender Debate

After deciding whether an Old English Sheepdog puppy or adult rescue dog is for you, the next thing on the list is to choose a gender.

Just like humans, Bobtails have different traits and characteristics that are gender-specific.

So to explore the gender debate, we need first to consider the typical physical and emotional differences between the two dog sexes.

Male versus Female

A male Old English Sheepdog stands approximately 22" tall at the shoulder compared to a female at 21". Males weigh 80-100 pounds while adult females come in at around 60-85 pounds and carry less bulk.

Both sexes are kind-hearted and fun-loving, but males tend to be the bigger clowns. While a female can be bossy, a male will never be far from his owner's side and tends to be clingier.

Surprisingly, male Bobtails are often more affectionate than females and are more likely to want to get up close and personal. When it comes to interacting with other household pets or their human family, female Bobtails are a lot more independent.

Regardless of this, though, if another member of the family, either two-legged or four-legged, is getting too much attention, a female Old English Sheepdog will muscle in on the act. As part of a pack or even as part of a two-dog family, she will attempt to hold the dominant role.

Not overly aggressive, a male will have a natural tendency to protect if he thinks it's called for. He will also have little hesitation at all in letting you know if you're not paying him enough attention.

Male Bobtails are known to have less of an attention span than a female, are less intelligent, not as quick to train, and less open to advanced training. It is male dogs, though, that are generally chosen for the show ring in conformation shows, largely due to their larger size and softer temperament.

Deciding Which Gender Is Better for You

Very often, breeders will recommend the male of a species, stating they make better pets. The reason for this is simple; the breeders want to hold on to the females (for breeding purposes). Therefore, it's in their best interest to steer potential buyers toward male pups. This fact may also be a consideration for you, depending on whether you want to breed from your female dog or offer your male dog as a stud.

So before you make your choice, consider your needs and situation and ask yourself a few questions.

- **Firstly, because males tend to be larger than females, will you find it easier to handle a female Bobtail?**

Female dogs shed blood when they come into heat. Male dogs not only mark their territory outside but may also do so inside the house, whether it's the corner of a room or the sofa. Which is the bigger concern?

Photo Courtesy of Aly Mui

- **Do you have another dog in your family who displays signs of jealousy? If the answer is yes, then opt for your new dog to be of the opposite sex.**

If your current dog has a medium aggression level with other dogs, then opt for your new dog to be the opposite sex. If, on the other hand, your existing dog has a low risk of aggression, either sex is fine.

A reminder, though; when you mix genders, you must make sure that either or both dogs are neutered or spayed.

You could also take into consideration other dogs in your proximity. For instance, if your neighbor has an aggressive dog, then you may want to opt for your new dog to be the opposite sex. It may sound extreme, but it could avoid a lot of unnecessary barking and fighting further down the line.

Is Two Company?

The short answer is yes, Old English Sheepdogs are great with other family pets outside of their breed, but there are riders.

First and foremost, and without sounding repetitive, is the need for training and socialization right from the offset. Bobtails love being part of the family, and if that includes other dogs or cats, then more often than not, that's fine with them.

It doesn't matter the size of your existing dog; as long as it's well trained and socialized, then your Bobtail will enjoy the canine company. The same goes for cats. If your cat is well-behaved and good around dogs then you won't have a problem. Remember, though a Bobtail is large and exuberant so you will need to watch them carefully around all small pets. It's easy for their clown-like behavior to result in them unintentionally hurting a small animal. They will even befriend bunnies; once again it depends on the behavior and temperament of each animal, but it is possible.

In fact, their gentle nature means they can easily expand their family circle to include all sorts of small family pets.

Raise your dog to be obedient and calm around other people, and he will be happy to share his space with other pets in his extended family.

Pairing Bobtails with other breeds of dog, depending on the type of dog(s), isn't generally an issue. Some breeds such as terriers or hounds, however, have strong fetch and chase instincts, which might cause a potential problem if you are bringing a Bobtail home.

Don't write any breed of dog off based purely on their preconceived breed characteristics, though. Canines are individuals, and in most cases, all breeds of dogs are only as good as their owners.

Don't Judge a Book by Its Cover

In my brother's chaotic household, Charlie, the bouncy Bobtail, joined a female Cocker Spaniel named Bonny. This unlikely duo lived and played cheek to jowl quite happily. The only time this combination became a problem was when Charlie accidentally rolled or sat his big rump on top of Bonny.

A discrepancy in size can also be apparent when you bring a Bobtail pup into a house with a small breed. Despite growing up to be a hulking lump of a dog, your Bobtail will believe himself to be the same size as his companion, and vice versa.

Yes, two is company, but timing, temperament, size, gender, breed, and age are key elements to success. Pairing dogs with too many similar characteristics may end in conflict while they struggle to establish their hierarchy.

The Reality of Adopting Littermates

The next dilemma you may be facing is whether to consider adopting two sibling puppies. You may, upon visiting the breeder, find it difficult to choose between two puppies and raise the question, "Why don't I take both?"

Some breeders will refuse to allow this or try to dissuade you. Meanwhile, less reputable breeders will see the profit before the welfare of you and the pups and will fail to fill you in on the huge commitment you are about to make.

There are some very good reasons why most breeders and dog experts are against the adoption of two pups from the same litter.

Two puppies are double trouble and are way too much work for the average family to cope with. Why? Apart from the obvious doubling of initial and ongoing costs, there are a lot of challenges you will without a doubt encounter.

Housetraining a new puppy is daunting enough. But when you have two pups, it's a whole new ball game. Just as you finish mopping up after one pup's accident, you will find his sibling soiling somewhere else.

You will need to have eyes everywhere. Young puppies need constant supervision. You could even find yourself preventing one dog from chewing your shoes while the other is happily at the other end of the room, destroying a throw cushion. If you work during the day, even part-time, then this is a real problem.

Some sibling pups bond to such an extent they prefer the company of their littermates to their owners. When this happens, it not only harms the bonding process, but it can also interfere with training.

On the flip side, some littermates can get jealous of one another and get into conflict.

Should you decide to go down the double trouble route, then you must keep the puppies apart for the majority of the day. You will need to schedule only two to three, 15-minute sessions of joint playtime each day. The pups will also need to be walked separately, trained separately, fed separately, and crated separately. Doing this will help the pups to bond with you, be open to training, and learn to exist independently of one another.

You will need to commit to this separation regime for 12-14 months until the dogs have formed their personalities and are confident individuals. If you don't do this, the dogs will grow into fearful and often aggressive dogs unable to exist independently of one another.

Within 12 months, these two cute puppies will grow into adults, so also ask yourself, is your vehicle large enough to transport two 60 to 100-pound dogs? Can you commit to allowing time for grooming both dogs? Do you have enough space in your home for two animals that size?

What's more, while it's very entertaining to watch two adults energetically throwing their considerable weight around, it can cause havoc indoors.

However, if you are set on wanting to adopt siblings and have lots of patience and experience, then there are a few advantages.

The first plus of adopting two puppies at the same time is – it's lots of fun! They can be very entertaining to watch while they both burn off all that excess energy.

Puppies will correct one another when playtime gets too rough. They do this by squealing when hurt, and this helps them to develop their bite control skills.

Their natural competitive instinct will help with recall. Call one OES, and the other is sure to follow. The same goes for other activities, including mealtimes. Once one hungry pup realizes it's food time and begins eating, the other will too.

Unfortunately, this desire to mimic one another's behavior can also be negative. Often when left to their own devices or when a visitor comes to the house, puppies will both bark. Littermates will become highly aware of anything they both believe is invading their territory. Often, even very quiet noises can trigger warning barks.

Before you make your final decision, remember; things may go well at first, but you always run the risk that it will ultimately result in disaster. And how then will you decide which of the two pups needs to be re-homed?

CHAPTER 3
Preparing to Bring Your Old English Sheepdog Home

"Old English Sheepdogs like to run and play. They need an active family with a good size home and a big yard to play. Old English Sheepdogs love spending as much time as possible with their family, so if someone works from home or can take them to work is ideal."

ANNETTE P SHORE
Carolina Shores

Photo Courtesy
of Pat and Kathryn Haran

Finding a Veterinarian

Once you have made the decision to make an Old English Sheepdog a member of your family, the first thing to do is find a suitable veterinarian.

You will need to take your new arrival to the vet soon after bringing him home, so begin your search with plenty of time and make your decision in advance.

Apart from vaccinations, regular check-ups, health issues, or even emergency treatment, at some stage in

FUN FACT

Tilley Brothers

Founded in 1881 at Shepton Mallet in Somerset, England, the Shepton Kennel for Old English Sheepdogs was overseen by brothers William Steeds Tilley and Henry Arthur Tilley. The latter was president of the Old English Sheepdog Club in England and founded the Old English Sheepdog Club of America in 1904. These brothers were instrumental in the early development of breed standards for the Old English Sheepdog breed.

their life, your Old English Sheepdog will need to visit a veterinarian. A suitable vet, therefore, should be local and readily contactable, if not on speed dial!

It is vital that you have a good working relationship with your vet. At the end of the day, you both have a common goal: the health and well-being of your Old English Sheepdog.

The first thing to do when looking for a vet is to make a list of the boxes your choice of veterinary practice must tick. For instance:

- Are you looking for a practice that supports or offers holistic and alternative treatments?

- Is it important to you that the clinic has cutting-edge equipment and facilities on-site?

- Are you more comfortable with a small practice where you will see the same vet every time you visit, or are you looking for a large set-up who may be more flexible with scheduling appointments?

- How far are you willing to travel?

- Does the clinic have parking facilities? Remember, you now have a large breed of dog, so accessibility could be an issue if your OES is unable to walk for any reason.

- Are the clinic's opening hours compatible with your work commitments?

- How important is it that the vet you choose is accredited? An accredited practice will have patient care standards.

Once you have contemplated these issues, the next step is to track down the right person to treat your Bobtail.

While your breeder or rescue center will have a trusted veterinarian, they may be too far away from your home address to consider. If this is the case and you don't have any doggy friends who can recommend a trusted

Photo Courtesy of Kelsey Silver

professional, the next port of call is the internet. Here, you can check out reviews and discover other pet owners' experiences and make a short list of any that you think could be suitable.

Failing this, check out the websites of local vets. They may have images of their facilities, resumés, a ballpark figure for treatment costs, and any specializations. The style and wording of the site will also give you a good insight into their work ethos.

Narrow the list down to a possible two or three and move on to the next phase: arranging a visit.

Even though you are flying solo, not having brought your pet home yet, the majority of reputable vet practices will be more than happy to accommodate you. Better yet, by calling first, you will get a good idea of the practice's customer service skills.

Once the appointment is made, get together a list of questions that you would like to ask:

- Can you tour the behind-the-scenes facilities, such as the treatment rooms and recovery areas?
- Are there separate waiting areas for cats and dogs?
- Is there a specialist referral system in place?
- What emergency treatments are available on-site, and if none, where will you and your dog be referred?
- Does the clinic have overnight patient facilities?
- Does the clinic offer an animal-collection service?
- Is testing such as blood work and X-rays carried out on-site or sent out to a third party?
- Does the practice offer payment plans in the event of your dog needing costly emergency treatment?
- Is there a pet insurance company that offers a specific discount for clients of the veterinary practice?

Don't be afraid to ask a lot of questions. Once you adopt your OES, your vet is very shortly going to become an important part of both your lives.

Having visited the practice, evaluate not only the response to your questions, but also take a moment to reflect on how the visit made you feel. Communication is an essential part of veterinary care, and if you don't feel at ease, you can rest assured neither will your Bobtail.

Did the vet and his staff make you feel comfortable? Were the surroundings relaxed? Did the office check all the boxes? If you can answer yes, then congratulations! You have successfully found the right vet for your Bobtail.

Identifying Hazards and Safeguarding Your Home

Dogs are nosy by nature. Once you add the elements of fun and curiosity present in Bobtails, it can lead to all sorts of problems for the unprepared owner.

Old English Sheepdogs don't remain small for long. Add into the equation their eye-covering bangs and characteristic clown-like behavior, and mishaps are inevitable. However, by safeguarding your home before you bring your dog home, you can ensure these accidents are not serious or fatal.

Photo Courtesy of Barb McNutt

Furniture and Appliances

- Be aware of furniture with sharp edges at head height, low tables with breakable ornaments, or tall lamp stands. If practical, in the early days, push floor-standing objects against walls as this will prevent puppies squeezing through narrow gaps and running behind furniture.

- In the short term, store any valuables or breakable objects.

- Consider a wall bracket for large-screen televisions. Look for any loose wires and cables, and make them safe with cable ties.

- If you have a home office, to prevent your OES from chewing important pieces of paper, wires, or cables, keep the door firmly closed at all times.

- Small pups may decide to climb into appliances, so keep doors to ovens, washing machines, dryers, and dishwashers closed.

- Will your dog sleep next to a fuel-fire heater, boiler, or anywhere close to an area where carbon monoxide may be present? Then make sure that all appliances are regularly and professionally maintained.

- Install child or dog gates where possible and screen windows. Keep doors leading to balconies closed.

- Take a good look at the flooring throughout the house. If your floors are shiny, cover them with non-slip mats.

- During the potty training period, if you have expensive carpeting or rugs, remove them where possible or cover them.

Food

Keep food in high cupboards or sealed containers. Don't be tempted to leave half-eaten food on plates, either. Be aware of food items that are toxic to dogs. Some of these include:

- Alcohol
- Apple seeds
- Apricot and peach pits
- Avocados
- Caffeine
- Candy and chocolate
- Cherry pits
- Chewing Gum
- Citrus Fruits
- Coffee and Tea
- Garlic
- Grapes
- Home Brewing Hops
- Macadamia nuts
- Moldy foods
- Mushroom plants
- Mustard seeds
- Onions, onion powder, garlic, and chives
- Peanut butter (if not Xylitol-free)
- Potato leaves and stems
- Raisins
- Raw or undercooked meat, eggs, and bones
- Rhubarb leaves
- Salty snacks
- Tomato leaves and stems (green parts)
- Walnuts
- Xylitol
- Yeast dough

Toxic Products and Choking Hazards

- Get into the habit of moving everything back from the edges of countertops. Although not known for it, adult Old English Sheepdogs are not beyond counter-surfing.
- Safely store all chemicals. These include kitchen, bathroom, and beauty products such as dishwashing liquid, bleach, bathroom cleaner, oven cleaner, window cleaner, laundry detergent, shampoo, conditioner, and more. Keep laundry, towels, and dish cloths out of reach too.
- Store all medication, pet or human-related, along with pesticides, in a locked cabinet.
- To prevent puppies from drinking water containing chemicals, keep the toilet seat closed at all times.
- Shoes and socks left lying around on the floor can be sucked and chewed. In a worst-case scenario, they are a choking hazard and can get lodged in your dog's intestines if swallowed. The same goes for small toys, which should be stored away and out of reach.
- Store plastic bags and trash bags safely as these are a choking and suffocation hazard.
- Chewing batteries can cause metal poisoning and chemical burns, so dispose of them responsibly.
- Keep coins away from pets as some are made using zinc, which is toxic when ingested by animals.

Create a Safe Space

By eliminating potential hazards before you even bring your new pet home, you can minimize the chances of future disasters.

Once your house is dog-friendly, you can decide on a safe space within a restricted area for your Old English Sheepdog to first settle when he arrives home.

Here, you can place his bed, crate, toys, and bowls. It is also where he will first meet the rest of the family.

Maybe you have a spare room or laundry room that is suitable. Alternatively, create a secure boundary using a baby gate.

Your chosen dog zone needn't be huge, but it should be quiet, enclosed, and comfortable. In the early days, it is ideal to limit your dog's access to the entire house until you have dealt with any unwanted behavior such as chewing or potty accidents.

Creating a Safe and Fun Outdoor Space

Your Old English Sheepdog is full of life, and apart from regular walks and exercise, he'll love spending time with you in the yard or garden. Before you bring your dog home, make sure that, just like the inside, his outside space is fun as well as safe.

- Some of the most common plants and flowers in your garden are toxic to dogs; these include:

- Aconitum
- Amaryllis
- Asparagus Fern
- Azalea
- Buttercups
- Crocus
- Cyclamen
- Daffodil bulbs
- Delphiniums
- Foxgloves

- Hemlock
- Hyacinth
- Hydrangea
- Ivy
- Laburnum
- Lily of the Valley
- Lupins
- Morning Glory
- Nightshade
- Oleander

- Pelargonium species of Geranium
- Rhododendron
- Rhubarb leaves
- Sweet Peas
- Tulip bulbs
- Umbrella plant
- Wisteria
- Yew

These will need to be removed or securely fenced off.

- Create boundaries to ensure your outside space is secure. You'll need to fully fence your yard or garden. Use sturdy materials and make sure that your OES's huge head can't get trapped between fencing panels! Ensure fences are over 6 feet high and strong enough to cope with a 60-100 pound dog potentially jumping up on it with its giant paws. Check that all gates have secure locks.

- Discourage your Bobtail from digging up plants by scattering the surrounding soil with hot spices such as dried pepper or mustard seeds. Bitter orange, rosemary, and sage will do the job too.

- Make sure that paints, chemicals, pesticides, poisons, cleaning products, petrol, fertilizers, antifreeze, etc., are locked away and out of reach.

- Fence off any cherished plants and flowers.

- All garden tools, including hoses, must be stowed safely away.

- Securely lock outbuildings, garages, playhouses, and sheds.

- Make sure your dog can't get into garbage and compost bins.

- Be aware that some types of mulch, such as cocoa bean shell mulch, are poisonous to dogs.

- Eradicate slugs and snails organically. Non-organic slug pellets and chemicals are harmful if your puppy or adult dog ingests them. If you think your Bobtail has eaten a snail or slug and appears ill, take him to the veterinarian immediately.
- Outdoor water features must be chemical-free.
- Fence off and securely cover Jacuzzis, hot tubs, ponds, and swimming pools.

Whether you have a boisterous puppy or an adult dog, making his outside space safe is essential. Remember, though, that until you get to know your Bobtail well, you should never leave him outside alone or unsupervised.

Photo Courtesy of Sharon Martin

Now you have made your outdoor space safe, let's take a look at a few things you can do to make it a fun place to play too!

Just Add Water: Add a simple water feature to your landscape that your OES can easily access. Consider a stream or splash-type fountain. Alternatively, why not build a small, shallow splash pool with gently sloping slides that your dog can easily get out of?

Paths to Success: Creating paths through your garden is a great way to keep your Old English Sheepdog stimulated.

Footloose and Fancy Free: Wherever possible, walkways and floor surfaces should be easy to walk on. Grass is ideal for pads but not so durable for heavyweight paws. Not to mention, if your dog pees on it regularly, you'll eventually have unattractive brown patches. Flagstones, concrete, and smooth rocks are great for walking on, as is mulch. Cedar and pine mulch is suitable; however, only use mulch products that are clearly labeled as being pet-safe. Your dog can choke on mulch, so he will need supervision if you opt for this type of ground covering.

Flower Power: Add interest to your garden with dog-friendly plants and flowers. Good choices include Cornflowers, Camellias, Honeysuckle, Lavender, Michaelmas Daisies, Roses, and Sunflowers.

Shade and Shelter: Due to their double coats, Bobtails can get very hot in warm weather, so make sure they have lots of shade and shelter. If you don't have trees, then investigate erecting an overhead tarpaulin or cloth shade that will cover a chill-out area. If this isn't possible either, a doghouse or plastic kennel is an option.

Play Safe: Choose a place in the outdoor space where your dog can let off some steam. Make it as large as you can. If you have lots of room, you can also consider creating an obstacle course for your dog.

Shopping for Success: Items to Have Ready

"Some OES are 'chewers' of nearly anything - plastic, rubber and wood are favorites. It is important to provide your dog toys to distract them from this behavior. A bored puppy is often a naughty puppy."

DEA FREIHEIT
SnowDowne Old English Sheepdogs

Before you bring your Old English Sheepdog home, you'll need to have some items on hand which you'll need from day one.

The list is quite extensive and, in terms of cost, can certainly mount up due to your Bobtail's eventual size and the care needed to keep his coat in tip-top shape.

Supplies you will need include:

- Food and Treats
- Feeding and Water Bowls
- Dog Bed
- Bedding and Towels
- Dog Crate (optional)
- Grooming Tools
- Toys
- Bitter Apple Spray
- Collars and Leashes
- ID Tag
- Car Harness
- Poop Bags, Newspapers, Kitchen Paper Towels and Hand Sanitizing Gel
- Canine First Aid Kit

Food and Treats: Your breeder or rescue center is the first point of contact for advice on the type of food your dog is used to. Find a local supplier that offers the same brand, or similar, and stock up in advance so it is ready and waiting when your new pup or dog arrives home.

In the first few weeks, it is better to keep your dog or puppy on the same kind of diet he was used to at the breeder or rescue center. If you wish to transition your dog to another brand or type of diet, this should be done gradually – ideally when the dog is settled in his new home and you have gotten to know him. Only then can you properly monitor any physical or behavioral changes to ensure your pet is responding well to the change in food.

Have a supply of dog treats on standby so you can begin training right away. You may also need both these items for your Bobtail's initial journey to his new home.

Feeding and Water Bowls: Opt for steel food and water bowls as they last longer. You may also consider buying a collapsible travel bowl for use on the move.

Dog Bed: Your new dog's comfort is paramount. Their bed is where they will rest and sleep, so be selective in your choice. What you're looking for is a good-quality bed that suits your budget. There are a lot of different dog beds on the market and it can be hard to choose. Here are just some of the available options:

- Donut Dog Bed: A round-shaped bed that is soft and cozy.

- Kennel Dog Bed: If you are intending to crate your OES, you could consider buying this type of bed. Some are designed for easy cleaning and are water-resistant. They provide a barrier between your dog and the hard floor. They are also useful for travel.

Photo Courtesy of Ailynn Knox-Collins

- Nesting Dog Bed: These have raised edges or rims and high sides with a deep space in the center where dogs can nest or curl up.

- Orthopedic Dog Bed: You may have adopted an adult or senior rescue dog that has musculoskeletal issues, in which case, this type of bed is ideal. It features special foam padding that conforms to fit the shape of the dog' body, helping to relive pressure on joints. It is ideal for hip dysplasia, a known breed-specific OES condition.

- Standard Dog Bed: these are usually round, square, oblong, or rectangular. They have no special features and come in a variety of fabrics and colors.

- Travel Dog Bed: Rather like a sleeping bag, this type of bed will either roll or fold for easy transportation.

Whichever type of bed you decide to purchase, make sure that you take into account the height, length, and weight of your puppy or dog. It may be advisable to opt for a less expensive nylon bed until you get to know your OES and ascertain whether he is a chewer!

The bed you choose should be large enough and strong enough to easily take the size and weight of your Old English Sheepdog. It may even be necessary to preorder the correct size and style bed from your local pet shop or buy it online. This is another reason why it is important to make a list and go shopping before the big day.

Bedding and Towels: You will need lots of comfortable bedding and towels, especially during the initial potty training stage. Inevitable accidents mean you will have to replace bedding quite frequently.

Dog Crate: If you have decided to crate your Bobtail, but have no crating experience, you may be unsure of what type of crate to purchase. Choosing the right size crate is extremely important if your puppy or dog is to feel relaxed. The crate should be large enough to allow the dog to stand and sit up tall. He should be able to turn around, lie down, and stretch out. Movement should be unrestricted. If you buy a larger cage than your puppy needs, he may view the crate as his toilet. To avoid having to buy a new crate every time your OES has a growth spurt, consider adapting an XXL-size crate by using a divider to section part of it off. By doing this, you can make the necessary adjustments as your dog grows. This way, you can buy a crate that will accommodate your dog once he is fully grown. You can find crates on

Photo Courtesy of Bonnie Goldsmith

the market that are capable of holding a dog of 90+ pounds. Opt for metal as they are a lot more durable.

Grooming Kit: Grooming an Old English Sheepdog is time-consuming and high maintenance. Begin by visiting your local pet store and investing in a good quality grooming kit.

This kit could include:

- A good-quality ground and polished pin brush (an oval brush of 9½" in length)
- A sturdy coarse comb with long round-top pins
- A medium-fine combination comb (for beard and ears)
- Fine-mist spray water bottle (pre-brush for a non-static coat)
- Nail clippers
- Pet shampoo
- Unscented pet eye and ear wipes
- Toothbrush and toothpaste
- A grooming table of 42-48" long by 24" wide, adjustable height if possible

The trademark shaggy coat and long fringe of the Old English Sheepdogs needs regular maintenance and will take a minimum of 30 minutes per day to tame.

Toys: Chew toys not only go a long way toward beating boredom, but they also help with dental and oral hygiene, soothe sore gums, and help with teething. Choose heavy duty toys that are designed specifically for large pets. They come in all shapes, sizes, and colors, so shop around.

Bitter Apple Spray: This preventative spray is a must when your Bobtail pup is learning the ropes. Bitter apple spray is cheap, available from all pet suppliers, and will prevent him turning your furniture legs into chew toys.

Collars and Leads: Measure your puppy or dog carefully to ensure that you get a correctly fitting collar and a leash suitable for your dog's size and weight. The collar obviously won't last him a lifetime because your Bobtail's neck is going to increase in width quickly. Whether you go for leather or nylon, though, just make sure it's a good fit and comfortable on his neck. The same goes for the leash; the older your Bobtail gets, the stronger it will need to be. Ensure it has a secure and easy to operate mechanism to attach to the collar. Avoid retractable leads, too, as they can jam easily.

ID Tag: Finally, something that will last a lifetime! With this in mind, buy a decent quality tag and make sure the contact details are correct. If you do move house though, don't forget to buy a new tag.

Car Harness: A Bobtail loose in the car is not a good idea, not only for his safety but also for yours. A harness will keep him safely in one place.

While some clip into rear seat belt sockets, others secure to anchor points in the rear luggage area.

Poop Disposal Bags: A must for when you take your Bobtail out in the world, or when traveling in the car. For your garden or yard, you will also need a poop-scoop! These range from simple plastic dust-pans to more sophisticated mechanical ones. Also, have a good supply of newspapers, kitchen paper towels, and sanitizing hand wash – you will need all the help you can get during the early stages!

Canine First Aid Kit: Buy a first aid kit from your vet practice or pet store, or create your own. Always make sure you have one readily on hand. In addition to the usual bandages and antiseptic cream, ask your vet about an emergency bloat kit.

Preparing for the Journey Home

If you're bringing an Old English Sheepdog home for the first time, it's natural to want to cuddle with him on the journey. Unfortunately, a dog loose in the car is neither safe for him nor the other passengers. Animals in moving vehicles should always be contained.

Why? Because allowing dogs to have free rein in a vehicle is dangerous. Your dog could climb out of the window, scramble into the front seat, or even distract the driver, causing him to brake suddenly and potentially crash the vehicle.

What's more, depending on where you're traveling from and to, different laws exist for dogs traveling in cars. It's a good idea to check on this with relevant government or state departments before you travel.

So, stay within the law and remember; dogs put their safety in our hands. We owe man's best friend a duty of care, no matter where life takes us.

You should always restrain animals using a dog-suitable pet carrier, travel crate, guard, or safety restraint. Therefore, a week or so before you collect your Old English Sheepdog from the breeder or the rescue center, take time out to dog and puppy-proof your vehicle.

Pet Carriers

If you're picking up a puppy, a fabric pet carrier bag is a good option. These bags are typically made from soft, yet resilient, breathable material with a reinforced base. They have handles that enable you to easily carry the bag and don't require a lot of storage space when not being used.

Place the puppy inside and zip the bag closed to prevent him from escaping. Multiple vented panels allow for proper airflow and also for your pet to see you. There may be a small opening to allow the puppy to peek his head out.

Pet carriers are a great way for you to be close with your puppy but have him safe and secure. Thanks to its small size, you can place the bag in the footwell or on the seat next to you.

What's more, they're versatile. You can also use the carrier to safely contain your puppy while visiting the vet. Or use the carrier if you need to take your puppy out with you before he's fully vaccinated and unable to walk on the ground.

Make sure whatever carrier you choose is suitable for your puppy's weight and size.

Travel Crates

Travel crates are typically made from thick plastic and have spring-lock, metal grid doors. They are one of the safest options when transporting a pet.

Dog travel crates are available in a wide variety of sizes, so whether you're collecting a puppy or picking up a fully grown adult, you'll be able to find a crate to fit your needs.

Photo Courtesy
of Joshua Morgado

A travel crate needs to be big enough for the puppy or dog to stand without his ears touching the "ceiling." He should also be able to turn around and lie down.

Large adult-size crates can be pricey, so make sure to take precise measurements of the dog before purchasing. Plus, don't forget to measure your trunk to check if the crate will fit inside with the door closed!

Although crates are one of the safest travel options, be aware that some puppies and dogs may react badly to a crate at first if they're not used to them. Travel crates work best when the dog is acclimated first before being locked in for a period of time. While a puppy may simply dislike the confinement and eventually settle, an adult rescue dog may become stressed or agitated. Remember, he may have had a bad experience in the past. If you're set on using a travel crate for your adult rescue, ask the center to test the dog in one before you pick him up.

Dog Guards

There are two types of metal dog guards; tubular and mesh. The name refers to the shape of the metal, whether it is in a grid pattern or takes the form of horizontal bars.

Both kinds of dog guards mount to the back headrests and prevent your pet from jumping from the trunk to the backseat. If you don't have a large enough trunk, many dog guards can be attached to front headrests, allowing your pet to sit safely and separately on the backseat.

Many pet owners like this option as it does not encroach on car or trunk space, and you can leave the guard in place. No need to lift and store large travel crates or risk forgetting to bring along harnesses or restraints.

Check out online options and order with plenty of time to allow for any returns if you need to purchase a different size or model.

Safety Restraints

Safety restraints typically take the form of harnesses for the dog to wear while sitting on a car seat with attachments that clip into your car's existing seat belt. They allow the dog to be free of the confines of a crate or pet carrier while still keeping them secure.

Generally, they work best for adult or placid dogs, who can stay still when traveling in the car. While the dog is not able to hop down from the seat or move around the car when he is restrained, he will still be able to jump up and down if he gets excited or agitated. Doing this could potentially distract the driver.

Some people may find restraints tricky to use at first, especially if you have an excited pup on your hands who is impatient to hit the road!

Extra Items to Have on Hand

Get a few items together for the journey home. What you need will depend on the length of the journey and the age and size of your Old English Sheepdog.

These items could include:

- Water and water bowl
- Collar and leash
- Dog chews and toys
- Blankets and towels
- Pet pads and newspapers along with kitchen paper towels
- Unscented wet wipes
- Plastic trash or poop bags
- Anti-bacterial hand gel

Pit Stops

Depending on the length of your journey home, you may need to make a few pit stops to allow your Bobtail to stretch his legs or take a potty break.

Adult dogs can hold their bladders and bowels up to five to six hours, while puppies can only hold for two to three hours. However, it's not advisable to make your new pet hold on for the maximum amount of time if it can be avoided. As a general rule of thumb, it's a good idea to take a rest from traveling every two hours for adult dogs and one to two hours with puppies.

Your OES will need small but regular amounts of water along the way, to prevent him becoming dehydrated.

Bear in mind, unvaccinated pups won't be able to walk in public areas or on the ground. In which case, you'll need to set down some puppy pads or sheets of newspaper for them to stand on and go potty. They also won't be able to walk and stretch their legs, but you can still carry them outside to get some fresh air and have a break from traveling in the car.

TOP TIP

If you have a long journey home, consider calling the breeder or rescue center ahead of time and asking them not to feed your new pet a pre-travel meal. For example, if you're picking up your pet mid- or late afternoon, ask them not to feed him breakfast. Doing this should help to prevent any travel sickness or diarrhea from nervous pups or dogs.

CHAPTER 4
One Step at a Time

Introducing Your New Arrival to the Rest of the Family

Bringing your Old English Sheepdog home for the first time is exciting, so it's only natural that the rest of the family will be eager to see him. If your new addition is a puppy, the breeder may have begun socialization, but bear in mind this is the first time your Bobtail has been separated from his mother and siblings.

Alternatively, if you have adopted an adult rescue dog, he may be cautious of his new surroundings.

Photo Courtesy of Tara Werner Padgetts Hill Puppies

Photo Courtesy
of Heather Virga

The journey home may also have added to your dog's anxiety, in which case, he will need you to introduce him to the rest of the family in the best way possible.

Ideally, arrange to collect your puppy or adult dog in the morning or early afternoon. This way, he will have longer to get used to his new home surroundings and hopefully be exhausted by bedtime!

Meet and Greet

First, show your Old English Sheepdog to his potty place and stay with him until he has relieved himself. It is essential from the very start to let your dog know where you would like him to pee and poop.

By now, you will have decided on a safe place for your Bobtail to sleep, eat, and play. So show your puppy or dog his bed or crate along with its comfy bedding, toys, food, and water bowls.

Give him time to explore his dedicated area and kneel alongside him while he has a good sniff of his new surroundings. His sense of smell is approximately five times better than yours, so he is going to be in sensory overload.

Once your Bobtail is calm, one at a time, invite a member of the family into the room. Ask them to sit down on the floor and speak softly in a reassuring tone. Wait for the puppy or dog to approach, and within a short time, he should begin to sniff, lick, and wag his tail. If, on the other hand, he shows any signs of anxiety, ask them to back away until he is ready.

Although close friends will also be eager to visit your new addition, this shouldn't take place until your dog is happy and relaxed in his new surroundings, and 100 percent at ease with his immediate family.

Take things slowly and look out for signs that your new addition is scared, in which case he may hide under or behind furniture or cower down. Should this happen, give him time to settle and don't crowd around him. Avoid sudden movements or loud noises and make sure the mood is mellow.

It can be difficult for adults not to get overexcited when they greet their new dog in a home environment for the first time, but for children, it's near

Photo Courtesy of Lisa Smith

*Photo Courtesy
of Amanda Vancheri*

possible! They will want to pick a puppy up and smother him, or in the case of younger kids, they may play too roughly with him. This is why it's vital to explain to children that a puppy is not a toy, and he may be tired or scared.

Children can often trigger a fearful response in a dog. They may pull a dog's ears or tail, or accidentally poke an eye. Their movements can be clumsy and they can inadvertently hurt a young puppy or even a mature dog.

An adult rescue dog is unknown to you, so watch out for any signs of aggression such as low growling, raised hackles, rapid panting, curled lips, teeth baring, wrinkling of the nose, or the pulling back of ears. If this happens again, have the family retreat and give the dog time to settle down. Don't be alarmed; he is probably frightened and just needs time to develop trust.

Allow him to slowly get used to the new smells, sights, and sounds around him. Maintain a quiet, calm, and stress-free environment, and use a soft voice until he is more at ease.

Naturally boisterous and excited children don't always understand why they can't play with their new dog on demand. Be patient and explain that to grow in confidence, puppies and adult dogs will need caring for and nurturing.

First impressions count and it's essential that this initial meeting with the family is as stress-free as possible for everyone concerned.

Photo Courtesy of Jennifer Noland

Creating a Workable Schedule for the First Few Weeks

Although a Bobtail pup is a blank canvas, he will be strong-willed. Therefore, the lessons he learns from day one onward are invaluable if he is to grow into a well-balanced, happy, and obedient adult dog.

Due to his young age, you can't immediately overload a puppy with rules, regulations, and advanced commands. You'll initially need a flexible schedule to guide him in the right direction.

A schedule is also imperative for an adult rescue Old English Sheepdog. You may not be fully aware of his background or the extent of any training he may have had, so the best way to allow him to settle within your household is to give him a routine to follow.

If you cannot be home all day during the first few weeks, it's a good idea to enlist the help of a dog sitter or member of the family who can step in.

A daily schedule will not only give puppies and adults mental stimulation, but also an idea of what is expected from them in the future. For a rescue dog, the certainty that he's going to eat twice a day, at set times, is welcome news indeed.

It's a good idea to write this schedule out and pin it to a notice board or attach it to the refrigerator so that all of the family can see what is needed and when.

These are foundations that you can build on to nurture a well-behaved and socialized dog that is a joy to own and a credit to both himself and you.

BEFORE BREAKFAST: As soon as your OES wakes up, take him outside to his potty place. Once he has relieved himself, indulge him with a short time of play and bonding.

BREAKFAST TIME: Feed your dog or puppy, wash out his bowl, and give him fresh water. Divide the daily total amount of food by the number of feeds you intend to give your dog. As a guideline, puppies will eat three times a day, while two meals is sufficient for adults.

TOP TIP

Check your dog's poop for worms and make note of its consistency too. Your vet will find any information you can give him helpful during your first visit.

Feed your dog around the same time each day. Don't be worried if an adult rescue Old English Sheepdog won't eat off the bat; it may take him time to adjust.

Photo Courtesy of Mary Eagon

AFTER BREAKFAST: Wait for at least an hour before exercising your dog; this will help to reduce the possibility of gastric torsion. When it's time, take him outside for a walk or into the garden or yard. Wait with him while he relieves himself. Regardless of whether he is a puppy or adult, do not leave your dog on his own.

Puppies can nap for as long as 14-18 hours a day, so post-breakfast is an excellent time for a nap. If your family has young children, make sure they don't disturb him while he sleeps.

Important Tip: If you take your adult Old English Sheepdog on a walk, do not let him off the leash. Keep him on the leash for the first few weeks, at least, or until you are confident of recall.

MIDDAY: If you work from home, now is the ideal time to have some quality time with your Bobtail. Puppies may want to play while adult dogs will particularly enjoy your company while you get on with your work. A rescue dog cooped up in a kennel has had little stimulation or human attention, so don't overload him all at once. Take this slowly and use the time to bond. Puppies and adults should once again be taken outside for a potty break.

LUNCHTIME: For pups, it's time to eat, followed by potty time. No exercise for puppies until an hour has passed, though.

For adult dogs, it's time for an outside play with supervision. Remember to give your dog fresh water.

MID-AFTERNOON: More play outside, a potty break, and a well-earned nap.

DINNERTIME: Time to eat for puppies and adult dogs. Repeat the process; eat, potty, wait an hour, exercise or playtime. Try to schedule this feed around the same time you eat your dinner. Begging and stealing food from your plate will follow if you feed your OES scraps from the table during the early days.

EVENING: Try to get your Bobtail to burn off as much energy as possible. A walk outside for adults or a run around the yard or garden followed by some quality time with the family while they watch TV or do homework. For puppies; lots of play, inside and out, along with a potty break. You will also need to take your adult dog outside for regular potty breaks too until he realizes that he must only relieve himself outside.

BEDTIME: Before bed, take your OES outside again for a potty break. Show him to his bed or crate, speak reassuringly, and settle him down for the night. Remember, if your dog cries, don't be tempted to allow him to sleep on your bed; it's a pattern you won't be able to break. Having a regular bedtime will help your dog to wake up at the same time each day. It is okay, though, during the first few weeks to place a dog crate alongside your bed for your puppy to sleep in. Line it with cozy blankets and drape one over the top to block out the light and help the puppy feel more secure.

While every dog is different, by setting a schedule for your Old English Sheepdog, you present him with the tools to settle in faster and be a wonderful addition to the family.

Great Expectations

"Think of your puppy as having the same needs as a human infant. They need to eat, drink water, go potty and get lots of rest. Don't take your puppy on outings to visit friends and family right off the bat. Let them settle in to their new home first."

DEA FREIHEIT
SnowDowne Old English Sheepdogs

Bringing your newly adopted puppy or adult rescue Old English Sheepdog home is an exciting and challenging time. For your Bobtail, though, the first few days can be confusing.

Knowing what you can expect during these days can ease any concerns you may have.

First of all, be aware that although you know your Old English Sheepdog is in his forever home, for him, the future seems unsure. Fortunately, you have done your due diligence and prepared well for his arrival.

By now, you have conquered the journey home and successfully introduced the new addition to your family.

So with **Day 1** under your belt, it's time to wake up and welcome in **Day 2**. **Day 2**:

The first chore of the day is to contact your chosen veterinarian and make an appointment for your Old English Sheepdog to have a health check.

Your OES may be curious, so while limiting your Bobtail's freedom, allow him to explore his immediate area. Don't be worried if he hides; take things slowly and at his pace.

Remember, though, supervision at all times and regular potty breaks every 2-4 hours. The same goes for adult rescue Bobtails too, who have been used to relieving themselves in their kennel. To your puppy, everything will be new, so be patient and understanding.

Day 3:

Every dog is different, so add any extra activities slowly during the first few days and respond to your Bobtail's body language. Continue on with regular potty breaks and stay calm if the odd accident, or three, happens!

If the first few days have gone according to plan, it's now time – while still keeping some areas of your home off limits – to allow your dog a little more freedom. As you become more confident of your Bobtail's behavior, gradually open up other areas of your home.

During the first 14 days, keep all doors closed and don't allow your dog to roam freely around the house. Puppies, and in some cases adult dogs, may

Photo Courtesy of Alicia Costner

not be used to stairs either, and while their natural agility means they can easily climb them, they may lack confidence when it comes to getting down!

Charlie wasn't introduced to stairs until he was at least a few months old. When he was, he loved going up them but enjoyed the game of barking until someone carried him back down a lot more!

Old English Sheepdogs are a fun-loving breed, and as they gain in confidence, their clown-like behavior will soon become apparent, and that's when all the fun really starts!

Lessons for Life

It is all too easy when bringing a Bobtail puppy into your home to feel that they've got their entire lives ahead of them in which to learn the house rules. Adopt a rescue Old English Sheepdog that you feel sorry for, and it's easy to be too lenient.

After all, a life expectancy of 10-plus years is a good number for a large breed. Along with this long lifespan comes a hefty weight of up to 100 pounds and the inherent ability to be strong-willed if not kept in check.

Schedules and ongoing training are the very foundations on which his lessons for life can be built upon.

Old English Sheepdogs are one of the smarter breeds of dog, and a schedule will let him know what's expected of him. Ongoing training throughout his life will also keep him mentally stimulated.

As with any large breed, the importance of laying the foundations for a well-socialized and obedient pup cannot be understated. Doing so will guarantee your Bobtail matures into a well-rounded dog that is a credit to both you and his breed.

Dogs aren't born misbehaving; they become so due to uncommitted, under-performing owners. Owning an Old English Sheepdog is no small feat. As a new owner, it is your responsibility to provide your dog with the guidance and instruction he needs if he is to become a valued member of your family.

CHAPTER 5
An Introduction to Parenting

The 411 On Crate Training

Dogs don't like to soil their dens so one of the main reasons for opting to use a crate comes down to its housetraining benefits. Crates are also useful for safely transporting your OES in your vehicle, as well as preventing him from chewing your furniture and possessions while you are out of the house. They are also a good way to isolate your OES from visitors who are nervous around dogs.

In the US, crating is a popular training method. However, that's not the case in all other parts of the world.

While some Scandinavian countries limit the length of time a dog may be confined, others like Finland ban it altogether. Crate your dog in Australia, and although not against the law, you're likely to face harsh criticism from your peers.

It's the misuse of crating by some pet owners that has led to criticism of this method within the dog community.

As mentioned, in the US, this way of training is a commonplace practice. If you want to crate your Old English Sheepdog, there are some important guidelines to observe. Following these guidelines will ensure crating remains a useful and positive training tool rather than a negative experience for your pet.

Size Matters

For an active, intelligent dog like a Bobtail, being confined for excessive periods can prove detrimental to his mental and physical health and adversely affect his socializing skills.

A crate is a training tool, and just like treats or clickers, it can be used as soon as your new OES puppy arrives home. As your puppy will grow to be a large adult dog, it makes sense to invest in a crate that he can grow into.

As a rough guide, an adult male Bobtail will stand around 22" at the shoulder. Allow an additional 20" of height to account for his head, plus some extra breathing room for good measure. The crate should also be large enough for him to stand up in and turn around easily.

As you can imagine, that's quite a sizeable crate. If you put your Bobtail pup in it from day one, it's going to swamp him. The answer is to purchase or make a divider that can be moved back incrementally to free up more crate space as your Bobtail grows.

A good quality crate will also come with a floor panel insert. Personal experience has pointed me toward plastic inserts rather than metal ones, as they're easier to clean in the event of an accident.

Photo Courtesy of Lisa Smith

Location, Location, Location

Once you have your crate, it is time to decide where to locate it in your home. Remember, the crate should be a calm and relaxing place for your dog to go and rest out of harm's way while still allowing him to see members of the family.

Bobtails are highly sociable and prone to loneliness when left without company for an extended period. Therefore, the ideal crate spot is in a quiet, draft-free corner of a high-traffic area of your home, such as the kitchen or living room. This allows your pet space while still making him feel like he is a part of the family.

Ensure the corner isn't close to a heat source such as a fireplace, radiator, or direct sunlight. It should also be clear of any dangling electrical cords or other potential hazards. See Chapter 3 for other in-home hazards.

Now that your crate is in the right spot, it's time to make it cozy. Old English Sheepdog puppies love to nest, so make sure your dog's bed is soft and comfortable enough to burrow into. He can also have his favorite toy in the crate with him as long as it's robust enough not to pose a choking hazard.

As your Bobtail gets older, his fur will become denser, which can increase body temperature. At this point, he may like a padded insert that is cool to sleep on.

Photo Courtesy of Jenifer Tuff

Introducing the Crate

Your Old English Sheepdog should view his crate as a positive space, a haven where he can rest and relax or seek comfort. It should not be a place he feels trapped or is reluctant to go inside voluntarily.

Some puppies and dogs may take to a crate immediately; others may need a little more help to get used to the idea. Either way, making use of rewards, specifically food treats, is a great tool to ease the process.

Step 1: Take your dog outside for a potty trip and wait until he has relieved himself. It is also a good idea to play with your dog, so he can use up any pent-up energy!

Step 2: Make sure the crate is inviting, filled with cozy blankets. Open the crate door wide and toss a few treats and toys inside for your dog to find.

Step 3: Bring your OES into the room with the crate. Sit nearby and allow him to walk around the room freely. As he gets closer to the crate, praise him and give him a treat. Once your dog has graduated to sniffing or placing a paw in the crate, throw a treat inside – your dog should follow. Once he is inside the crate, do not shut the door; instead, give more praise and feed him treats while inside. At this point, it is good to introduce a cue word, such as "crate," when he enters. Repeat this process for a few days or until your pet is no longer wary or suspicious of the crate.

Step 4: Once your Bobtail has become comfortable with the crate and associates being inside with treats, his next step will likely be sitting or lying down in the crate. When he does this, use your cue word "crate" and wait a few moments to give him a treat. This teaches him that it is remaining in the crate that earns the reward rather than merely entering. Place the treat on the crate floor. Do not feed the treat to him from your hand. If the dog leaves the crate, do not give him a treat.

Step 5: After following Step 4 for 1-2 days, it is time to begin weaning your pet off the treats. Make the transition from him responding directly to bribery, to following your voice cues and training. Continue to use your cue word "crate" and praise your pet when he enters, but do not reward him with a treat every time.

Step 6: Now, it is time to build up the amount of time your dog spends in his crate by increasing the amount of time he must remain in the crate before receiving a treat. Use your cue word "crate" to call your puppy inside. Wait 5 seconds before praising and placing a treat on the crate floor. Allow your puppy to leave the crate completely before calling him back inside. Now, wait for 10 seconds before rewarding him. Continue this process, increasing in 5-second increments until your puppy is happy to sit in the crate for a whole minute.

Step 7: Your puppy should now be comfortable sitting inside for a whole minute; next, you must ease him into being inside with the door closed.

Photo Courtesy of Joanne Smith

Call "crate" when your dog enters and sits, then close the door but do not latch it shut. Reopen the door immediately and reward your dog with praise and a treat on the crate floor. Allow him to leave the crate completely before repeating the process.

OES IN FILM
Please Don't Eat the Daisies

An Old English Sheepdog made an appearance on the set of the 1960s sitcom *Please Don't Eat the Daisies*. The show, based on a book and movie of the same name, follows the Nash family, including their four sons, maid, and large sheepdog.

Step 8: As with Step 6, begin to increase the amount of time your Bobtail must remain in the crate with the door closed, but not latched, before being rewarded. Like before, build up in gradual 5-second increments, allowing the dog to exit the crate before re-calling him. When you are confident you and your pup have mastered this step, begin latching the door when closed.

Step 9: Repeat Step 8, but now when you latch the door, take one step backward before reopening it and rewarding your dog with a treat. Once your dog is comfortable with you moving back a step, begin increasing the amount of time you wait before stepping forward and reopening the crate door. As always, build up gradually in 5-second increments.

Step 10: Using the same method as laid out in Step 9, slowly increase the number of steps you take away from the crate and how long you wait before opening the crate door. Continue this step until your dog is calm and comfortable with you moving all the way back to the room's exit. Do not rush; ensure you have truly mastered this step before moving on.

Step 11: Now you can call your puppy into the crate, calmly latch the door, and slowly leave the room. Wait 60 seconds before reentering, opening the door, praising, and rewarding. Gradually increase the amount of time you wait outside the door, beginning with 30-second increments until you can leave the room for 5 minutes. Then build up in 60-second increments until you're able to leave him for 30-60 minutes.

Step 12: The final step is to begin adding distractions to teach your puppy to remain calm in the crate, even while there is another activity going on in the room. Begin with simple things, such as sitting in the room reading a book, while your dog remains in his crate. As he loses interest in what you are doing, increase the activity level to calmly walking around the room or cleaning up a little, then after a while turn on the TV or put on some music. You can also gradually increase the number of people in the room.

The above steps are applicable to both puppies and adult dogs. The only difference is that you will need to keep a closer eye when crate training

Photo Courtesy of Danette Moseley

a rescue OES. He may have had a negative past experience with crating or confinement in general. If he becomes agitated or distressed at any time during the crate training process, hit the pause button. Seek advice from your veterinarian or rescue center before continuing; it may be that you need to consider an alternative method.

Limit the Crating

It goes against a dog's natural instinct to soil his own den. Taking your puppy for a potty trip outside before and after he enters and leaves his crate will aid house training.

Be mindful that puppies under 6 months have tiny bladders and short attention spans, so should not be crated for more than 3 hours without a bathroom break. As your puppy grows up, he will be able to hold his bladder for longer, but even so, an adult dog should not be confined for longer than 6 hours at a time.

As your Bobtail matures, his time in his crate with the door closed will ideally be restricted to overnight. However, there may also be situations when you need to crate him for short periods during the day too. For example, when running errands or hosting new people or children in your home.

Daytime crating for short periods (around 1-2 hours) is not detrimental to your pet. But confining 100 pounds of bouncy Bobtail to a crate all day while you're at work is inappropriate. A dog that lacks sufficient exercise and human interaction is likely to become anxious and depressed.

If you are away from home during the day, and do not wish to leave your Bobtail to roam free, consider hiring a pet sitter. Alternatively, enlist the help of a family member, or take your dog to a daycare facility.

Top Tips for a Positive Crate Experience

- Purchase a crate large enough for your puppy to grow into and use a divider to customize the crate size as time goes by
- Plastic inserts are preferable to metal ones for ease of cleaning
- A crate with two doors will give you more flexibility in terms of where you can position it in your home
- Use treats to make being in a crate a positive experience for your puppy
- Take your puppy outside for a bathroom break before and after crating, and every 2-3 hours during
- Never use the crate as a punishment
- Don't lock up your Bobtail for excessive periods during the day
- Don't give your dog meals or water in his crate

Home Alone: How to Cope with Separation Issues

"One of the best things to have for the first few nights is a towel or blanket with their mothers scent on it. This will help comfort the puppy."

ANNETTE P SHORE
Carolina Shores

It's true what they say; dogs really are man's best friend. The bond between a canine and his owner is like no other, which is why your new pet is likely to feel upset when you have to leave him home alone.

This feeling is natural, and a lot of dogs are able to self-soothe after a short period and will wait contentedly until you return home again. However, some dogs may display more dramatic behaviors in response to you leaving and are unable to calm themselves.

If so, your OES may have separation anxiety, which is a serious condition that requires careful managing, so as not to become a long-term issue.

Signs your Old English Sheepdog may be suffering from separation anxiety:

- **Howling and Barking:** Howling or barking that is relentless and persistent, triggered the moment you leave or show signs of leaving the home.

- **Urinating and Defecating:** If your dog is housetrained and does not usually have accidents while you're together, then urinating and defecating indoors while you are out is a common symptom of separation anxiety.

- **Chewing, Digging, and Destructive Behavior:** Scratching at exit points, such as doorways and window frames, and chewing and destroying household objects. Note that this is only a sign of separation anxiety if the dog does not usually do this when you are in the home. This behavior is particularly dangerous, as your pet may injure himself, either by damaging his nails, breaking his teeth, or hurting his paws.

- **Escape Attempts:** Dogs that become severely distressed when left alone will often attempt to escape the home or yard. Again, this can potentially result in injury.

- **Pacing:** Pacing back and forth in straight lines or a circular pattern when alone is a common coping mechanism for dogs who are feeling very anxious.

Identifying the Cause of Separation Anxiety

Animal behaviorists don't fully understand why some puppies and adult dogs are more prone to separation anxiety than others. However, several factors can trigger separation anxiety in your OES. Being aware of these factors is essential if you are to avoid aggravating your pet's condition.

Here are some common scenarios which can trigger an episode of separation anxiety:

- **Being left alone in the house for the first time:** If you have taken time off work to bond with your new puppy or adult Bobtail, the day will come when you have to return to your regular routine. This will be a difficult time for your OES, who has grown accustomed to having you around. The same goes if you typically work from home and take a new job that requires you to work outside of the house.

- **Change of owner or guardian:** This scenario is more applicable if you have adopted an adult rescue OES. The process of leaving the rescue center, having already potentially been abandoned for one reason or another, can cause old anxiety to resurface in a dog.

- **Moving house:** Moving to a new house can trigger separation anxiety too, even if your dog did not previously display signs.
- **Loss of a family member:** If a family member is suddenly absent, whether they have passed away or moved out of the home, it can lead to the development of separation anxiety.

Photo Courtesy of Jenna Waltz

Photo Courtesy of Meghan Nikituk

Finding a Solution

How you manage your OES's separation anxiety will depend on how severe his symptoms are. It is also a good idea to have a chat with your veterinarian. Double-check that your dog's behavior, such as urinating or pacing, is not caused by an underlying health condition.

For mild cases, one of the best approaches is counter-conditioning. This method involves replacing an undesirable behavior with a desirable one. To do this, you need to teach your OES to associate something positive with the disliked situation.

- Before leaving, make sure your Bobtail has had plenty of exercise and playtime. A tired dog is more likely to settle into sleep.

- Each time you leave home, give your dog a special treat. This can be a Kong-style toy filled with kibble, a silicone mat spread with peanut butter, or a simple dog-safe bone. Whichever treat you use, reserve it only for when you go out. When you return home, take the treat away.

- Try to make your exit and entrance as low-key as possible. Avoid a drawn-out goodbye with your Bobtail. Instead, opt for a calm and straightforward "see you later," as you leave. Establishing a set phrase that you use every time you go and return will, over time, reassure your dog that you are coming back. When you return, wait a few minutes before calmly and briefly greeting your pet.

- Leave your OES with an item of clothing or blanket with your scent, as it will comfort him.

In more severe cases, it will take more than a treat to distract your OES from his anxiousness. You will need to gradually make him feel more comfortable with being alone so he can unlearn his panic response to your departure.

- In severe cases, your OES will begin feeling anxious before you even leave the house. He may react to simple actions like you putting on your coat or picking up your keys. When you are in the house and not planning to leave, go to pick up your keys a few times. Put on your coat or shoes, but then go to sit at the kitchen table. Doing this multiple times a day will eventually stop him from associating these actions with you leaving.

- Most of a dog's anxiety about you leaving the house stems from his fear that you will not return. Teaching him that you will always come back is the best way to minimize his anxiety. With your puppy or dog in his safe place, tell him to "stay." Pick up your keys or put on your coat and then leave the room, shutting the door. Wait only 1 minute before returning. Repeat the process, waiting an extra 30-60 seconds before returning each time. Once you have built up to around 5 minutes, continue on with this method, but this time leave the house entirely before quickly returning. Then build up the time gradually as before. Continue with this process until you feel confident that your dog is comfortable with you leaving and staying gone.

When you have addressed and treated the root cause of your Old English sheepdog's anxiety, you can continue with simple distraction techniques, as outlined previously.

What Won't Help

Whether you have welcomed home a new puppy or adopted an adult rescue, coping with separation anxiety can be stressful for both you and your Bobtail. Although this can be a stressful time, you mustn't punish your dog for acting out when you have to leave the house. Remember, his response is born out of fear, not rebelliousness.

Dealing with Unwanted Puppy Behavior

"If you don't want them doing something as an 80+ lb. adult, don't let them do it from the beginning. For example, while it is tempting to hold your new puppy on your lap on the sofa, you may not want your adult dog on your lap. Another rule of mine is: four paws on the floor or you don't get pet."

DEA FREIHEIT
SnowDowne Old English Sheepdogs

In order to have an adult Bobtail that is a well-mannered and obedient companion, it is necessary to put in the work while he is still a puppy. By nature, puppies are playful and curious; the way they learn is by pushing their boundaries to see what is and isn't acceptable.

In nature, for example, if a puppy bites his mother too hard, she will snap at him to teach him this is wrong. As the puppy's new human parent, it is up to you to set the boundaries of what is appropriate behavior in your household. A puppy will only get away with what you choose to allow.

While you may feel tempted to delay disciplining during the early days so as not to upset the initial bonding, it is essential not to let unwanted behavior go unaddressed.

Correcting unwanted behavior needn't turn into a negative experience for you and your pup. Remember, a puppy who understands his boundaries and knows what is expected of him will grow to be a more happy and well-rounded adult.

So, what exactly is an unwanted puppy behavior? The most common examples are chewing household items, barking and whining, and biting and/or nipping. As the saying goes, prevention is better than cure. So we will look at ways to try and stop these behaviors from happening in the first place as well as how to address them if/when they arise.

Photo Courtesy
of Melissa Solis

Chewing

Chewing is a very typical puppy behavior. From the ages of 4-7 months, your OES will lose his milk teeth, replacing them with adult teeth. As with human babies, this can cause pain and discomfort. Often a puppy will try to relieve this pain by chewing. However, chewing can also take place due to boredom. Regardless of the reason behind your pride and joy destroying your brand new slippers, it's important to rectify this behavior now, so your puppy doesn't carry this habit into his adult years.

First, try to prevent your pup from eating your favorite household items by making sure he has plenty of chew toys to mouth on. During the early days, just after you have brought your puppy home, limit his access to only one or two safe spaces or rooms, and aim to keep him well supervised at all times.

If you find your puppy chewing on an item he shouldn't be, tell him a firm "no," and immediately replace it with one of his own. Praise him when he returns to chewing his own toy. If you come across an item that has already been chewed, but you did not catch your little tyke in the act, do not try to show him the object of your annoyance and discipline him. His attention span is very short, and he won't understand why he is in trouble. All you will achieve is making him feel scared or anxious. Keep in mind that during these first weeks, you don't want to hinder the bonding process. Stay calm and aim to keep a more watchful eye on your Bobtail in the future so you can nip unwanted behavior in the bud as it happens. You may want to monitor your pup's behavior by installing a pet camera. These allow you to broadcast your voice when you catch the dog doing something he shouldn't!

Barking and Whining

You may find one day that your Bobtail suddenly wakes up and "finds his voice." Your once shy and timid new family member is now a vocal and confident puppy. In some respects, barking can be a positive sign. It shows that your puppy is integrating well into the family home and growing an attachment to the people in it by wanting to protect them. However, excessive barking can become a more serious problem. This is especially the case if you are living in an apartment or close to unforgiving neighbors.

What's more, if your dog barks continually, it will become increasingly difficult for you to learn to decipher between your dog's different barks and what they mean. You may accidentally dismiss your dog when he's trying to tell you he needs to go outside to the bathroom or warning you that there's a stranger at the door.

In most cases, a puppy will bark and whine out of boredom or to get your attention. Therefore, ensuring you set aside enough time to play and interact with your new OES is essential. By tiring him out and spending quality time with him, you may be able to prevent the issues from occurring.

If your pup is still overly vocal despite your best efforts, it's time to teach the "quiet" command. First, quickly assess the situation. Ensure that your dog isn't displaying any sign of being in pain or isn't trying to get outside to the bathroom. If neither seems to be the case, avoid shouting at your dog when he is barking or whining. Shouting can escalate the situation as he assumes you are joining in. Instead, tell him "quiet" in a firm but calm voice. Wait until his barking ceases, even it's only while he catches a breath, and immediately give him a treat and praise. After several repetitions, he should learn that following the command "quiet" to stop barking or whining results in something positive.

You may have heard it is best to ignore a puppy barking or whining completely and pay him no attention. However, this advice is more tailored to adult dogs rather than puppies. Barking can give your dog an adrenaline rush, which can cause him to associate barking with feelings of excitement. Puppies learn by pushing their boundaries until they are told something is unacceptable. So, by not commenting on their barking and ignoring it, you can inadvertently teach them that there is nothing wrong with this behavior.

If your puppy is barking or whining specifically while in his crate, you may have rushed through some of the crate training steps, moving on before he is comfortable being inside with the door locked. Revert back to **The 411 on Crate Training** and repeat some of the steps until your dog feels calm and safe inside his crate.

Biting and Nipping

Puppy biting and nipping is not always a sign of aggression. This behavior is often how they play with their siblings, relieve teething pain, and explore the world around them – much like babies! While this behavior is natural and expected, it is still essential to curb this habit, so your puppy does not take it into his adult years. Tiny milk teeth nibbling on your hand may be amusing now, but a giant Bobtail mouth chewing on you can be painful and may potentially be a gateway to aggressive biting.

Bite control is an essential lesson for your puppy to learn. Many behaviorists believe that a puppy that has learned to control his jaw is less likely to cause serious harm. So if he ever does bite someone, it will be in response to an extreme scenario and one where he is in pain or danger.

During the time spent with his siblings and mother before leaving the breeder, your puppy will have begun to learn bite control. If he nipped his mother too hard or got too boisterous with his siblings, they would likely have snapped at him until he stopped. As the dog's human parent, you must continue and build on this work by teaching him not to chew his human family members. Here are some important Do's and Don'ts when it comes to breaking the habit of biting and nipping.

Do's	Don'ts
The moment your puppy begins to mouth you, immediately replace your hand or foot with one of his own chew toys	Don't avoid playtime with your puppy in an attempt to limit nipping. Playtime is a crucial part of the bonding process. It is far better to address the behavior rather than merely trying to avoid situations where it may occur.
If your puppy tends to nip or mouth you when you stroke or scratch him, try distracting him by feeding him little treats while you pet him. Doing this will help your puppy get used to being touched without mouthing you back.	
Encourage types of play such as fetch and tug of war that are non-contact. Once your puppy has learned to enjoy these games, try carrying a tug toy or ball around the house. When your puppy begins to bite or nip at you, immediately try to engage him with his tug toy or the ball.	When your OES puppy mouths or nips you, do not suddenly jerk your hands or feet away. It can cause him to become more excited and maybe even try to grab on tighter. Instead, allow your hands or feet to go limp and unresponsive.
Keep buying exciting new toys for your puppy; this will prevent him from becoming bored with your distractions.	
Arrange playdates for your pet with other fully vaccinated puppies either through your friends or family. Alternatively, join a puppy class so your dog can continue to socialize and learn from other puppies in a supervised environment. This will further his understanding of what are and aren't acceptable levels of boisterousness during playtime.	
If you don't have a distraction toy on hand when your puppy nips at you, let out a high-pitched yelp as soon as you feel your puppy's teeth on your skin. Immediately walk away and ignore him for 30-60 seconds. If your puppy continues to nip, leave the room for 30-60 seconds again, and then return.	Never slap, shake, or hit your puppy even if he hurts you with his nipping. Physical punishment can cause your puppy to become afraid of you and result in aggression.
Consider using a spray deterrent such as Bitter Apple and spritz it on your hands and feet. When the puppy begins to nip at you, stay still and calm and wait for him to react to the nasty taste. Continue doing this until your puppy ceases his nipping.	

Keep Calm and Carry On!

When dealing with any unwanted behavior, the most important thing to do is remain calm. Your puppy could interpret an angry or aggressive response as encouragement or you joining in with the play. Instead, keep your body language slow and deliberate, and your tone of voice firm but calm.

Furthermore, never reprimand your pet after the behavior has already occurred if you were not present while it happened. You will only confuse your pet and may cause him anxiety, which can negatively impact your early bonding experience.

And So to Bed

In the same way you wouldn't expect to get a decent night's sleep straight after bringing a baby home, you need to be prepared to become a night owl until the fluffy new family member settles into a routine.

Most puppies leave their breeder, and therefore their mother and siblings, at around 8 weeks old. The excitement of meeting his new family and exploring a new home may distract your Bobtail from this separation during the daytime, but the nighttime is a different story. In the quiet and dark, it is natural for a new puppy to become anxious, at least until he comes to realize that he is safe and not alone.

Like many new puppy owners, my brother Steven chose to crate his OES puppy Charlie at night, following the breeder's advice. Crating at night is an excellent aid in bedtime training. It keeps your puppy safe while you're asleep, preventing him from wandering around getting into mischief, but he's also more likely to warn you he needs to use the bathroom. Puppies typically don't like soiling their sleeping area. Crating is also a way you can keep your puppy close by during the night without bringing him onto the bed.

Creating a calm and positive bedtime routine will help to ease your pup's transition from his dog family to your human family.

Before Bed

It goes without saying, a tired puppy is more likely to fall asleep easily and quickly. However, it's not quite as simple as making sure your OES has lots of daytime exercise. He will likely nap all afternoon and then come back to life in the evening with bundles of energy.

A couple of hours before you plan to go to bed, make sure to spend lots of quality time playing with your pup. Try to include games that are stimulating both physically and mentally. As an example, you can use hide and seek or name training games where your puppy receives a small treat for running to the family member who calls his name.

Take your puppy outside to the bathroom before bedtime. Try to speak to him as little as possible, and when you do, use a calm and quiet voice to make it clear this is not playtime. No matter how much patience it takes, wait with your puppy until you can be sure he has wholly relieved himself.

Bring your puppy's crate into your bedroom during the first few nights, at least. Position the crate next to your bed, where your puppy can easily see you. If your breeder gave you a towel or blanket with his mother's scent, put that inside. It may be a little stinky but will bring your pup lots of comfort and make him feel safe. The smell will fade gradually and be replaced with your home's smell, so it is a fantastic way to ease him gently into his new environment. If you do not have an item from the breeder, use one of your worn T-shirts as this will also help with the bonding process.

Arrange some puppy pads, newspaper, or even a trash bag under the crate to protect your bedroom floor just in case of an accident. It's also a good idea to keep some wet wipes on hand in case your dog is sick in the night.

In Bed

Do everything you need to do before bed, such as brushing your teeth or changing into pajamas, before bringing your puppy into the bedroom. It is best for family members to do this in turns and with a minimum of fuss. If the whole family suddenly disappears to the bathroom and begins changing their clothes, your puppy may get the idea something exciting is happening or that you're about to leave the house.

Once you are ready for bed, calmly bring your puppy into the bedroom. If he is wearing a collar, remove it, and place him in his crate. Immediately switch off the light and get into bed. Try to go straight to sleep, or at least pretend to, without reading or watching TV. With any luck, your pup will get the message, and after a few minutes of realizing you're being no fun and not playing, he will do the same and go to sleep.

Unfortunately, it is more likely that he will whine or even bark. Try silently placing a hand on his crate to let him know you are there. If the whining continues, in a very soft, gentle voice, comfort your puppy.

During Charlie's first few nights at home, Steven's wife, Becky, my sister-in-law, would even sing him a children's lullaby, which is a trick I carried on with when I adopted my first Great Dane puppy.

Whatever happens, don't be tempted to get your puppy out of his crate and cuddle him. If you took him to the bathroom before bed, gave him sufficient food and water during the day, and have him next to you so know he isn't in danger, you can attribute this whining to your puppy simply not wanting to go to sleep yet.

Try to hold out as long as you can; your OES will eventually tire out and fall asleep. Once you have let the whining continue for a long time, it becomes even more important not to give in and cuddle your pup or let him onto the bed. Doing so teaches him that persistence is the key to success. Remember, how you handle this first night will set the tone for all the nights to come. Staying strong through one sleepless night to let your puppy self-soothe is far better than giving in and dealing with sleepless nights for weeks on end.

A 2 to 3-month-old puppy can typically hold his bladder for 3-4 hours. Therefore, if you sleep around 8 hours at night, you should expect to take him for 1-2 bathroom breaks during the night. You can either rely on your puppy to wake you up to tell you he needs to go or set the alarm to wake yourself up to take him outside.

When taking your pup for a middle-of-the-night potty break, silently remove him from his crate and, if at all possible, try not to turn on the bedroom light. Carry him outside and set him down. Do not speak; it needs to be very obvious this isn't playtime. Stand in one spot and wait patiently for him to relieve himself. If you must talk to him, do so in a quiet, gentle tone. Once he has been to the bathroom, praise him just once and take him straight back inside. Return him to his crate, still in complete silence, calmly close the crate door, and get back into bed.

As your puppy gets older, his bladder control and capacity will increase. As a rule of thumb, a puppy can hold his bladder for as many hours as months of his age plus one. So, a 6-month-old puppy should make it for 7 hours through the night.

The Morning After

Puppies, like kids, don't like sleeping late! There is simply too much important playing to be done to wait patiently in bed come morning time. It is best to accept that you will have to become accustomed to waking up earlier during these first few weeks. Chances are, though, if you get up early to take your pup outside, feed him, and spend some time playing and cuddling, he will collapse not long after. This means you can both get in some much-needed napping!

The Call of the Wild

The first few nights will likely be a little challenging. It is completely normal for your puppy to feel anxious and scared during this transitional period, and it is not a reflection on you.

In the wild, a puppy separated from his mother is more at risk of being attacked by a predator. In order to discourage their mother from leaving them, puppies whine and cry. To keep them quiet, she stays close by and limits her time away from them as much as possible. You may know that your puppy is safe and cozy in a warm crate at the foot of your bed, but his natural instinct doesn't tell him yet.

As your puppy becomes more confident and settled, you can move the crate out of your bedroom if you so wish, but make sure to do this gradually.

Teaching Old Dogs New Tricks

Most of the information in this chapter relates to bringing a new puppy home. So, what if you adopted an adult rescue OES? Unless the rescue center gave you a detailed account of your Bobtail's past, you can't assume that he is fully housetrained just because he is an adult. Therefore, as with a puppy, you may still need to put in a great deal of time training or retraining him.

Take It Slow

While the general idea is the same, the physical process of housetraining will differ a little. A puppy will have led a sheltered, trauma-free life with his mother and siblings. While puppies will have some anxiousness due to a sudden change of home, their resilience and eagerness to please means they can settle quickly and take on new instructions.

Photo Courtesy of Morgan Dennis

An adult rescue OES, however, not only needs to learn new behavior to meet your expectations, but, in doing so, must potentially unlearn old behaviors from his previous family. Therefore, training needs to take place at a much slower pace and requires a very watchful eye. In your dog's last home, "training aids" such as rolled-up newspapers, feet, hands, chairs, and sticks may have been commonplace if he did not respond to instructions. As a result, training sessions might trigger a feeling of panic or fear. Tread carefully and make sure to keep your body language neutral and voice firm, but never raised when giving instructions.

Crate training is still an option providing your rescue OES has no issues with confinement (the rescue center should be able to provide you with this information). You can follow the same steps for crate training as you would with a puppy, but take longer with each step before moving on. It's essential to ensure that your dog is comfortable before upping the ante of the training.

You should never try to push a rescue dog outside of his comfort zone; it may trigger a negative response and undo all of your hard work while also causing him severe stress. For this reason, it's a good idea to get to know your rescue dog better first and let him settle into your home before you begin training. Once you have formed a bond with your dog and observed him in your home for a few days, you will be better equipped to notice if he shows signs of being stressed or feeling endangered during training sessions.

Senior Dogs

You will undoubtedly have heard the phrase, "You can't teach an old dog new tricks." Does this mean you shouldn't bother attempting to train a senior rescue OES? Certainly not! In fact, along with Labradors and Golden Retrievers, Old English Sheepdogs are hailed as one of the most highly trainable dog breeds.

A study undertaken at the University of Vienna discovered that senior dogs might need twice as many repetitions and corrections than 6- to 12-month puppies when undergoing training. However, the senior dogs actually outperformed the puppies in logic and reasoning tasks. The study also found that a dog's age had no impact on his ability to retain the information once he had learned it.

A Lifelong Commitment

The prospect of training an adult rescue OES may seem daunting. While you do need to be mindful of his potentially negative past, you should never underestimate a dog's resilience and ability to adapt and overcome. If you set reasonable expectations and goals, training can be a positive experience for both you and your rescue Bobtail. If his previous owners were neglectful or abusive, having a clear picture of what is expected of him and receiving praise when he acts out that behavior will be a gratifying feeling for him.

CHAPTER 6
Training Basics

Potty Training 101

Don't let the words "potty training" strike fear in your soul. Yes, potty training can be a long and, at times, messy process, but it's not as challenging as some would have you believe.

The key is to begin potty training right away and remain vigilant to prevent accidents before they happen. During the early days, try to anticipate when your puppy may need to go to the toilet and create a schedule.

Photo Courtesy of Cindy Barkle

Photo Courtesy
of Angela Biber

Creating a Schedule

As mentioned previously, puppies are generally able to hold their bladder for one hour plus an extra hour for every month of their age up to around 9 months. This would mean a 3-month-old puppy should be able to hold his bladder for 4 hours. However, certain activities can throw a wrench in the works and mean your puppy needs to go to the toilet more frequently.

To prevent accidents, you should take your puppy for a potty break:

- Immediately after waking up in the morning or from a nap
- After indoor playtime and training sessions
- Before entering and immediately after exiting his crate or bed
- Within 5-30 minutes of eating or drinking
- Before bedtime or naptime
- Immediately after chewing a toy/bone

While your puppy is still small, it may be useful to pick him up and carry him straight outdoors. This will prevent him from making a potty pit stop in your house on the way to the door. Make sure always to use the same door and take him to the same designated "bathroom" area.

In the initial stages, it's also a good idea to leash your puppy when you set him down outside. You can then guide him to the specific area where you want him to relieve himself. After a while, the scent in this particular area will likely prompt him to go. Leashing your pup also prevents him from wandering around and becoming distracted from the task at hand.

Here are some further signs that can indicate your pup needs to go potty!

- Intently sniffing the floor or carpet
- Suddenly wandering away from the family
- Walking or running around in circles in a specific area
- Whimpering
- Running to a door
- Becoming overexcited

As your puppy grows older, his bladder capacity and control will improve. Once he has learned where he is allowed to relieve himself, he will be able to take himself to the bathroom, providing the back door is left open, or tell you when he wants to go outside.

Praise and Reward

When you take your puppy outside to the bathroom, stay with him until he has relieved himself. Stand still and remain quiet, gently holding the leash. Once you see your puppy squat down, just as he is about to go, say "go potty," or another cue word of your choice. When your puppy has finished, immediately shower him with praise and reward him with a tasty treat.

Photo Courtesy
of Annemarie and Paul Philips

Photo Courtesy
of Kelsey Silver

Unleash your puppy and remain outside for a few minutes to play with him. Doing so teaches your pup that the quicker he does his business, the faster he can get to the fun part! Returning inside immediately after your puppy has relieved himself may teach him that it is better to stall before going to get more quality time with you.

Do this every time you take your puppy for a potty break, and soon enough, he will even look forward to doing his business outside!

Accidents Happen

Like human children, puppies can't be perfect all the time and small accidents may happen. If you catch your puppy in the middle of peeing or pooping indoors, say a firm "uh-oh" to get their attention, maybe even click your fingers. Focus on sounding firm, but do not shout or raise your voice – you don't want to scare your pup. Immediately pick him up and take him outside. If he finishes his business, immediately praise and reward him as you usually would.

FUN FACT
Bagel the
Therapy Dog

Bagel the Old English Therapy Dog has led an exciting life. From somewhat humble beginnings as a therapy dog in Los Angeles, she rose to stardom with her role in The Little Mermaid Live! as Max, Prince Eric's dog. You can follow Bagel's adventures on Instagram @ bagel_old_english_therapy_dog.

Return to the soiled area and clean it thoroughly to eliminate any residual odors. If you do not clean the area sufficiently, it is likely your puppy will be drawn back to this spot and repeat his mistake.

As frustrating as indoor accidents can be, never punish your Bobtail if you didn't catch it happening at the time. Once the accident has occurred, and your puppy has scampered away, it is too late to administer a correction. Taking your puppy back to the scene of the crime and rubbing his nose in it can cause him to become nervous about going to the toilet in front of you. As with all training, excessive punishment or scolding only serves to reverse any progress you may have made.

Homemade Stain Removal Recipe

A white vinegar solution will neutralize urine odor and works well on wet stains.

- Begin by blotting the soiled area.
- Mix equal parts of white vinegar and cold water. Pour the solution over the soiled area.
- Blot well and allow the area to dry.
- When the area is entirely dry, vacuum as usual.

Crating and Potty Training

If you have decided to crate your puppy and begun the process of crate training, rest assured that doing so will also aid your potty training endeavors.

As previously mentioned, dogs are naturally clean creatures, and it goes against their instinct to soil where they sleep and nest. For this reason, your puppy is highly likely to whine, bark, or scratch at the crate floor when he wants to get out to the bathroom. Keep an ear out and take him straight out to the yard. Try not to delay, as once your puppy has had an accident in their crate one time it is far more likely to happen again.

To prevent a crate accident, ensure that the crate is not too large. If your puppy has too much room inside to move around, this can encourage him to use one corner as a bathroom. If you purchased a large crate for your puppy to grow into, make sure to partition off excess space.

Photo Courtesy
of Jill Kelpin

Housetraining an Adult Dog

Thanks to the saying "You can't teach an old dog new tricks," many people believe that housetraining an adult or senior dog will be much more challenging than with a puppy. In fact, in some ways, it can be easier. Adult dogs have increased bladder and bowel control and capacity, meaning they can go for more extended periods without a bathroom break. This makes it more manageable to monitor and avoid accidents in the house. It doesn't, however, mean that you don't have to remain vigilant or can skip a few steps.

There are a few reasons why an adult rescue dog may not be housetrained:

- His previous owners never took the time to train him
- He may have only ever lived outdoors
- He may have spent a long time confined in a crate or cage, where he had to relieve himself in his living space
- He has separation anxiety, and the sudden change of environment is causing him to urinate indoors

When welcoming an adult rescue dog into your home, it is best to assume you are starting from scratch. Even if your rescue OES was housetrained previously, a refresher course will help him apply those lessons to meet his new home's expectations.

Follow the same method as you would for a puppy:

1. Take your dog out regularly (after waking, before entering or after exiting his crate, after mealtimes, after intense play or training time, after chewing a bone/toy, before bedtime).

2. During these times, leash your OES and take him straight outside to prevent a mistake on the way to the door.

3. Use the same door and take him to the same outside spot each time.

4. Keep the dog leashed and wait silently with him until he does his business.

5. When he finishes, shower your dog with praise and reward him with a treat.

6. Do not return inside immediately, but rather spend some quality time outdoors once the dog has been to the toilet. Just 10 minutes will suffice.

7. If you catch your dog relieving himself indoors, make a sound to catch his attention. Immediately lead him outside and praise him once he has finished his business outside.

8. Never discipline your dog for an indoor accident you did not see happen.

9. Watch out for circling, pacing, whining, or purposeful indoor sniffing; they can all be signs your dog needs to go to the bathroom!

The only difference you may experience in housetraining an adult Bobtail rather than a puppy is that when taking him outside this frequently, he may not need to go every time! Wait patiently, and if after a long period he doesn't seem to need to relieve himself, take him back inside. Do not let him walk freely around the house, but instead put him in his safe, confined area such as his crate. Wait for 10-15 minutes before trying again.

Adult or senior rescue dogs are more sensitive to punishment. As a result, it is best to remain as vigilant and cautious as possible to prevent accidents before they can occur. Keeping the process as calm and positive as possible will yield far better results.

Photo Courtesy of Collen Becker

Discipline and Reward, Explained

"OES are very smart. Remember almost all misbehaviors are 'operator' error, meaning YOU did not set up your dog for success. Leaving food on the counter and then getting mad at the dog when they eat it, not taking them out frequently enough to go potty and then they have an accident are both examples where it is the humans fault, not the dogs."

DEA FREIHEIT
SnowDowne Old English Sheepdogs

Before we delve deeper into training your dog to perform specific acts, it is beneficial to have a clear understanding of the behavioral science on which most dog training is based.

The Basis of Training

B.F. Skinner, a well-known behavioral scientist, performed several experiments in the 1950s. From these experiments, he was able to conclude a number of principles that can be applied to all living creatures with a central nervous system.

Skinner deduced that animals are more likely to repeat behaviors that are rewarding or enjoyable to them. Conversely, they are less likely to repeat an action that results in something undesirable, i.e., discipline or punishment.

Neutral stimuli, things that don't matter to that animal, don't impact behavior either way. As humans, we can make use of these findings by applying them to dog training.

Old School versus New School

Most pet owners who hear the word "discipline" take it to mean something negative that involves physical punishment like smacking, kicking, or jerking the lead. In modern-day training terms, just as a "reward" can be anything that your dog enjoys, like food treats, praise, or playing ball, "discipline" or "punishment" is simply something that causes your dog to decrease a specific behavior.

In the past, training using physical forms of punishment, also known as "alpha training," was popular. An example of alpha training would be to knee a dog in the chest to prevent it from jumping up to greet you when you enter the house. Now, such practice is greatly frowned upon by most major dog and animal organizations. The American Veterinary Society of Animal Behavior has publicly voiced concerns that such methods can be ineffective and dangerous. Furthermore, it can damage the relationship between the owner and dog as well as inhibit your dog's enthusiasm for training.

These days, most dog training focuses purely on positive methods with the means of discipline being punishment by removing attention. What does this actually mean? Let's return to the example of managing a dog who jumps up every time you walk through the door. As you walk through the door and your dog begins jumping up, turn your back on him and don't make eye contact. This removal of your attention and affection would be the "discipline" or "punishment." When your dog ceases jumping, begin praising and petting your dog as his "reward" for stopping the undesirable behavior.

The Problem with Punishment

The main issue with the physical punishment training model is that to change the dog's behavior and stop it reverting back, the punishment needs to increase in intensity over time to prevent desensitization.

Desensitization is a common occurrence because dogs trained with negative punishments merely inhibit a specific behavior to avoid a punishment they don't like, rather than learning an alternative positive behavior. The dog often doesn't understand why he is being punished, which can lead to depression, aggression, and a higher tendency to bite.

There is a lot of room for error with punishment training. The dog may come to fear the punishment associated with a particular situation rather than his specific behavior or reaction to it. For example, if he pulls on his lead when he sees another dog, and he is punished with a sharp jerk on a tightening collar, the dog may come to associate the negative punishment with seeing other dogs rather than realizing it's related to his behavior of lunging. In the future, his reaction to unfamiliar dogs may become more aggressive because he is associating seeing other animals with impending punishment.

A Rewarding Experience

Reward-based training with non-physical discipline is hailed as a safer, more enjoyable, and scientifically supported approach. Chapter 8 of this book will explore further training options that don't use physical punishment but are based on Respect Training.

CHAPTER 7
The Importance of Socialization

"We've found that it's best to introduce them to only one dog at a time, be sure that this happens in a controlled environment. Short periods of play are better than long periods to start with."

ANNETTE P SHORE
Carolina Shores

Photo Courtesy
of Michele Parker

Helping Your OES Understand His Place in the Family Dynamic

In the 1940s, animal behaviorist Rudolph Schenkel carried out research collected from studies on a pack of captive wolves. His results, simply put, suggest that there's a hierarchy in which the alpha (leader) maintained the group through aggressive and dominant behavior.

As dogs are believed to have descended from wolves, it was assumed that this pack dynamic also related to domestic dogs. Domesticated dogs are not wild wolves, though, and more recent studies have called these findings into question.

FUN FACT
Winner!

Old English Sheepdogs have won Best in Show at the Westminster Kennel Club annual dog show twice (as of 2020). The first OES to win was named Slumber and took home the champion title in 1914. The second was Sir Lancelot of Barvan in 1975.

Why? Because in the wild, wolf packs are made up of a male and female couple and their offspring. As the wolves mature, they leave their family and create their own packs. A large part of Schenkel's study was brought about by studying captive wolves. Here, multiple captive adult wolves of the same age were housed together. This scenario is not something that would occur in the wild, and therefore the validity of the research is flawed.

There is, however, a social hierarchy among canines, which is something you can capitalize on when making a dog a part of your family. A dog will naturally recognize a leader. If a dog lives with a family made up of a mother, a father, and a child, it will see the child seek permission from its parent and go to him or her. You don't need to force your OES to become submissive to you and see you as a dominant figure, but you must provide guidance, leadership, and direction.

By nature, dogs rely on their owners to lead, protect, and provide food, water, and shelter, plus love of course! Not taking time to fully understand your role as the "parent" of your OES is setting you and your Bobtail up to fail.

From 12-16 weeks of age, a happy, cared-for puppy will be at ease in his new home. While some pups are confident, born leaders, others may be more timid and prefer to follow. One thing they all share in common, though, is the need to survive. This instinct may lead to a more submissive dog feeling that in the absence of a suitable head of his family, he has to

Photo Courtesy
of Michelle Johnston

take up a leading role. Assuming a role he doesn't want, but feels he must fill, can cause a dog a great deal of stress.

For this reason, your dog must see you as head of the family.

To do this, you must first follow a few simple guidelines:

- Set clear standards of behavior for your Bobtail from the moment he becomes a part of your family.

- Be reasonable in your expectations.
- Be clear and consistent, and make sure all other family members are too.
- Devise a daily routine and make sure you and your family keep to it.

Once your dog realizes that you are in charge, you will have a happy household.

Here are some pointers to make sure your OES knows his place in the family dynamic:

- Always eat first before feeding your OES.
- Go through any doors or gates first. Your dog must learn not to push his way through; he must move out of your way.
- Take your place on the sofa first. If you allow your OES on the couch, he must understand that it's only acceptable when you say it is "okay." The same goes for getting into the car, in his crate, going outside, etc.
- Set a daily routine from the moment your dog wakes up to the time he goes to bed. You say when it's time to cuddle, play, enjoy a treat, etc.

Your dog will challenge you from time to time. He may decide to bark or nudge for your attention, push in between you and loved ones, or counter surf. All of these things may seem cute when he is a fluffy puppy, but not so much as a large adult. Observe your dog's behavior carefully from the very start and decide which ones are acceptable to you and your family dynamic. Let him know and understand his place through non-violent behavior without the need to intimidate or dominate. Do this, and your dog will feel safe around an owner that is calm and consistent in the role as head of the family.

Photo Courtesy of Susan Montgomery

Photo Courtesy of Stacie Bryant

The Importance of Socializing Your Dog

By nature, Old English Sheepdogs are affectionate, loyal, and protective of those they love. Due to their large size and rambunctiousness, they must be socialized early on in their development. Bobtails love to be the center of attention and can easily knock older people or children over with their clowning around.

While the breed by and large is polite and likes the company of other animals and meeting new people, some OESs can be timid if not correctly socialized from the outset. The world will be a little less scary once your dog gets used to venturing outside his home. Daily walks along different routes are the secret to success. It is also a good idea to take your puppy out at different times of the day and evening. Remember, though, that before a full course of vaccinations, you must carry your puppy rather than allow him to walk on the ground.

Start this from an early age and introduce your Bobtail to adults, children, and other animals and continue it throughout his whole life.

Introduce Your OES to Different Experiences and Environments

Take your puppy out for short trips in the car. Car journeys should not be solely for visits to the vet or boarding kennel; make it a happy experience too.

Depending on where you live, take your Bobtail to the train or bus station, airport, forest, or the beach. Mentally stimulate your pup's brain and engage his senses with new smells, noises, and sounds.

Build his confidence with trips to the shops. Do this by starting small and working your way up to the mall. Take your Bobtail for coffee, or to dog-friendly events. Introduce him to different floor surfaces, including grids, cobblestones, wooden flooring, marble flooring, gravel, carpet, sand, and more.

Also familiarize your dog with cars, trucks, street furniture, bicycles, skateboards, strollers, wheelchairs, shopping trolleys, and any common everyday object he is likely to come across on his daily walks.

Consider enrolling your OES in puppy training classes. This is an excellent way to introduce your puppy to other dogs and a great opportunity to get you out and about with like-minded people.

Photo Courtesy
of Linda Gallagher

Socializing with Other Dogs in Public Places

Dogs are everywhere, so it's a sensible idea to get your puppy used to interacting with other canines.

As you are meeting other dogs outside of the home, keep your puppy on the leash. This will avoid him coming into direct contact with any dogs that may not be fully vaccinated. Be aware that just because another dog is in a dog park or with his owner, doesn't mean he's well trained or socialized. The last thing you want is for your puppy to have a bad experience.

Photo Courtesy
of Adam Jory Waxman

Photo Courtesy
of Skyler Jokiel

Some dogs are scared of others and can become more fearful on a leash because they feel they can't escape the focus of their fear, and so their second instinct is to fight.

It is relatively easy to identify if your puppy is afraid of other dogs.

- He may lunge, bark, or snap at other dogs.
- He may excessively yawn or lick his lips.
- He may attempt to retreat from the new dog or even hide.
- He may whine or shiver when another dog comes close.
- He may refuse to interact with or even take treats around other dogs.

If you suspect your puppy is scared of other dogs, you must first eliminate any fears he may have. You can do this in several ways.

- Be aware of your dog's personal space. See how close is too close to another dog. It may be 5 feet or 50. Once you have established this distance, never allow your dog to get any closer until you are confident you have addressed his fear.
- Change your pup's perception of other dogs. Make your Bobtail believe that other canines at a safe distance mean that something good is about to happen. When a dog comes into view, give your puppy a rapid succession of his favorite dog treats, one at a time, until the other dog is out of sight.

- As your puppy's confidence grows, gradually decrease the distance between your puppy and other dogs. For example, if your OES's comfort zone is 10 feet, reduce it to 7. If it's 5, cut it to 3, and so on.

When your pup is brave enough to meet other dogs, start by taking things very slowly, and maintain control. Allow the dogs to meet one another by circling and sniffing for no more than 30 seconds. When you are both happy with the encounter, slowly walk away from the other dog. As soon as you are out of sight, reward your dog with a treat.

As a dog owner, it is your responsibility to make sure that other dogs are safe around your pet as well as different types of animals. From cats to cows and hamsters to horses, aim to get your Old English Sheepdog used to seeing other species.

While he is on a leash, walk your puppy around places where he is likely to encounter other animals, large and small. Follow the same steps that you would with a new dog, and in time, your Bobtail will become well acquainted with the rest of the animal kingdom.

If you have adopted a rescue OES, ask the shelter or previous owner about the dog's history. Find out if he is aggressive, fearful, or excitable around other animals before introducing him to new experiences.

If he is, follow the same steps as those for a scared puppy.

Photo Courtesy of Ashley Calhoun

Meeting New People

If your dog's interaction is restricted only to those in his family, he may become wary of anyone outside his immediate circle. For this reason, it's vital to take him out to meet and greet other humans.

It's good to introduce your Bobtail puppy from the ages of 8-16 weeks to as many different people (men, women, and children) outside the family as possible.

Diversity is key, so allow your Bobtail to meet and greet a wide range of people. Get him used to people from all walks of life, in different sizes, ages, ethnicity, and personality.

Here are some effective ways to achieve this:

- Encourage new people to touch, play with, and give treats to your puppy as calmly and gently as possible.

- Make sure that while petting your puppy, strangers touch him on his chest, chin, or somewhere else their hands remain visible.

- Provide dog treats for strangers to give to your dog. This will help to make meeting new people a positive experience.

- Watch for tell-tale stress signs. These may include excessive panting, yawning, shifting weight to the rear legs, dilated pupils, drooling, and licking. If this happens, remove your dog from the situation without comforting him – this enforces fear – and take him to a quiet place to regroup.

- Ensure that the time spent interacting with new people is long enough to get acquainted without tiring your OES puppy out.

After 18 weeks, it will become a lot more challenging, although not impossible, to socialize your dog. So don't despair if you have rescued an OES.

You can do this just as you would with a new puppy by reading your adult dog's body language for stress signs. Also, look out for defensive behavior, which may be a result of negative past experiences.

These signs may include barking, lunging, snarling, or growling.

If you see any of these signs, you may need to enlist the help of a professional or join a specialized dog class.

However, if your rescue dog is unsure rather than defensive about meeting new people, you can go it alone by keeping new encounters short and sweet. Once you learn how to read your rescue's behavior and prevent him from becoming stressed, he will quickly relax and learn.

Photo Courtesy
of Kathleen Herman

Tips on Combining A Multi-Pet Household

Just like family members, occasionally pets don't get along either. While this is a challenge, it isn't cause for concern or a reason to change your plans of adding another pet to your family.

Are you planning to open your home to pets of the same species or combining dogs with a household of cats, horses, hamsters, birds, or rabbits? Whatever your aim, you have to remain faithful to a strict set of ground rules.

When you bring your puppy home for the first time, existing pet dogs generally react in one of three ways.

1. The existing pet dog will be hostile

2. The existing pet dog will tolerate the new addition as long as he doesn't get in the way or encroach on his space

3. The existing pet will accept the new addition and start to bond with him almost immediately

While most pets get to this in around an hour, some may take longer. So, to help ease the process, begin by making a formal introduction.

As your puppy will not have received his full vaccinations, it won't be possible to take the dogs to the park to meet on neutral ground. In this case, place the puppy in a crate, and allow the existing dog to look at and sniff the new addition. The existing dog must not have any direct physical contact with the puppy, though.

When the puppy is not in a crate, keep him in a closed room where he is safe.

Interaction between the pets should be monitored and supervised at all times. Try to keep these interactions calm and friendly.

Remove any pet toys belonging to the existing pet to avoid conflict and ensure that both animals can easily retreat to their crate or bed.

Follow these steps until you are confident the dogs are getting along. When you are sure they are, and not before, you may give both animals the freedom to roam.

The same rules apply for an adult rescue dog, the only exception being that both pets can be introduced to one another in a neutral place outside of the home while on a leash.

If you have more than one existing pet, then follow these steps, one animal at a time, to avoid the puppy feeling overwhelmed.

Feline Fine!

Introducing your puppy to your cat may be a bit trickier. Some cats can be suspicious of other species entering their home environment.

The best way to begin is by introducing the pair to one another through a gate or door.

If you can't do this, then place the puppy on a leash and allow the cat its freedom to escape. You must give the cat the upper hand to decide if he wants to make friends.

Again, keep the animals separated until they are either happy with or indifferent to one another.

Horse-Play

If you own a pony or horse, then your Old English Sheepdog needs to learn how to get along with him.

If your Bobtail is a puppy, carry him up to the horse and allow each animal to sniff one another.

Ask another member of your family to hold the dog and allow him to watch you and your horse interact with each other. Ensure that whoever is in charge of your Bobtail is calm and rewards the pup with treats and praise.

Doing this early on in the relationship can prevent your OES from getting overexcited and jumping up or chasing the horse. It's essential to not only prevent any nasty accidents but also to make sure the two animals are not fearful of one another.

Your Family and Other Animals

To socialize your new OES with small animals, such as snakes, birds, rabbits, hamsters, hamsters, and parrots, first secure the animal in its cage or tank.

Place the puppy on a leash and get out his favorite treats. If you are introducing an adult dog to your small pet, you may need to use a muzzle.

While keeping a tight hold of the leash, walk your dog slowly toward the cage. If he doesn't make a lunge for the cage or tank, calmly praise your dog and reward him with a treat. Doing this is a simple way of reinforcing his good behavior.

On the flip side, if your Bobtail displays any signs of aggression, pull him gently but firmly away from the cage or tank. He will soon realize that by being aggressive, he won't be able to walk in his chosen direction. Once your dog is calm, walk back toward his cage and repeat the positive reinforcement. You will need to practice this many times, and maybe even over a couple of months. As you progress, reduce the number and frequency of the treat.

You must not let your OES off the leash around other pets until you are 100 percent sure of his ability to behave.

Dogs that begin by chasing and killing small animals can find the experience stimulating. So socializing your puppy or dog to accept small animals is well worth the effort.

How to Avoid a Feeding Frenzy

Always keep pets away from one another's food bowls. Firstly, they may have different dietary needs or be taking medication, but also it helps avoid spats.

When pets share food bowls, it is also impossible to make sure they are each getting their recommended daily amounts of food. This can result in a pet being either overweight or underweight.

Also, while your puppy thrives on his food, it may not be suitable for an adult dog or cat. When possible, feed each pet in a different room or at opposite ends of the feeding area. If you can't separate the animals, then stay with them while they eat and make sure each one is keeping to his food bowl. Pick up and remove any uneaten food.

CHAPTER 8
Progressing from Beginner to Advanced Training

Setting Realistic Goals

As a breed, Old English Sheepdogs respond well to training. They are successful in the home and the show ring. However, although loving and obedient, they still need to learn to curb their natural impulse to herd and chase, be it cars, animals, or people!

Also, Bobtails grow at an alarming rate, which means they must be fully trained by the time they reach young adulthood. A dog this size can cause a lot of damage around the home if not properly schooled.

Once your dog has grasped the basics, it's time to look toward more advanced training. For this large breed, obedience training is a must even if

Photo Courtesy of Lisa Wright

it only includes the most straight-forward commands such as "stay," "come," "sit," and "leave it."

The first step toward starting your OES on the road to advanced training is setting realistic goals for your new dog and yourself. Decide how much time you are realistically going to commit to your dog's training needs, devise a program, and, most impor-tantly, stick to it. When it comes to training, consistency is king.

Remember when you set your goals that obedience train-ing can open the door to a whole new world of sporting activities that are ideal for your athletic and versatile Bobtail.

TOP TIP

When my brother Steven started Charlie's advanced training, he wrote out a checklist of what he wanted to achieve weekly and monthly. He wrote down everything that Charlie had learned. He said that doing this helped him plan out the following week's schedule and motivated him when things weren't going especially well or not according to plan. This is also something that older children might enjoy getting involved in too.

Dog Commands

Once your realistic goals are set and you have decided on a schedule and program, it's time to decide which commands you want to teach your Bobtail.

Before you do this, though, first decide where you intend to carry out his initial training. Ideally, this should be in a quiet area with no distractions. You can progress to command training your dog in a public place after a lot of practice in your home or yard and when he is focused on the task at hand.

Here are 12 verbal commands that you may like to consider teaching your Old English Sheepdog:

1. "Sit"	**5.** "Come"	**9.** "Crate" (or "Bed")
2. "Stay"	**6.** "Drop It"	**10.** "Out"
3. "Down"	**7.** "No"	**11.** "Wait"
4. "Heel"	**8.** "Leave It"	**12.** "Okay"

When you are ready to begin training, remember, you will need to be patient while carrying out sessions at regular intervals. Keep sessions short and simple. You don't want to push your Bobtail too hard at the outset. At the end of the day, command training should be fun for both of you.

As soon as he has grasped one command, move on to the next, and reward him with praise and treats as you progress.

Photo Courtesy of Bill Zehrung

So let's begin!

1. "Sit"

This command is one of the most important to teach your OES. It will provide your dog with the skills he needs to ask for things he wants. Better yet, it will encourage him to remain calm and controlled.

You can teach this command by putting a dog treat close to your Bobtail's nose. Slowly move the treat upward. He will follow it, causing him to lift his head high and he will naturally adopt a sitting position. Issue the command

"Sit" and give him the dog treat along with lots of love and praise. Repeat the process until he learns the command. This command is useful when you later take your dog for a walk as it can prevent annoying interactions with other people or animals.

2. "Stay"

First, ask your dog to "Sit." Put the treat close to his nose and issue the "Stay" command. Take a few short steps away from your dog. If your dog stays and waits, give him the treat. If he doesn't, say "No" and a few at a time, take a couple more steps away from him. You will need to repeat this exercise 6-8 times every day. The good news is that learning this command will help to improve your Bobtail's self-control.

3. "Down"

This puts your Old English Sheepdog in a passive position, which means it can be a challenging command to teach. You will need your dog's favorite strong-smelling treat in your closed hand. Move your closed hand containing the snack close to his nose, and the second he catches its scent, move your hand to follow. Your dog will follow. Next, move your closed hand along the floor to encourage him to follow the treat in a lying down position. The moment he is "down," issue the command word and quickly reward him with the treat. This command is useful for when you want your OES to lie on his bed or rest close to you. Plus, it's a way to settle your dog when you have visitors or are eating.

Photo Courtesy of Cathy Hausman

Photo Courtesy
of Stephen Gosling
Stephen Gosling Photography

4. "Heel"

Make sure that your OES learns to pay attention to you when you are out walking by teaching him the "Heel" command. You can teach your Bobtail this command by taking his leash in your right hand with him positioned close by on your left side. Place you left hand on the leash also so you can keep your OES close. Holding treats in your left hand, command your dog to "Sit." Next, command your dog

HELPFUL TIP
OESCA Rescue

The Old English Sheepdog Club of America (OESCA) maintains a directory of rescue contacts and organizations curated by their rescue chairperson. A regionally sorted map and list can be found at the OESCA website: www.oldenglishsheepdogclubofamerica.org/Rescue/

to "Heel" and begin walking slowly. As you walk, continually feed your dog small treats from your left hand. After several repetitions, building up distance each time, gradually reduce the frequency of treats you reward your dog with as you walk until your OES will walk to heel without treats.

5. "Come"

Put a collar and leash on your Bobtail. Walk a specific distance from your dog and ask him to "Come" toward you, while gently pulling on his leash. The second your dog comes to you, reward him with a treat. This way, he will get the idea of what is needed from him. Repeat this exercise every day, several times. When you want to release the dog, say "Okay" and give him lots of love and praise. This command is one of the most important to teach an Old English Sheepdog. It will prevent him from getting into trouble should he begin to chase anything in the park or street.

6. "Take It" and "Drop It"

Hold your Bobtail's favorite toy in one hand while at the same time provoking him to grab the object of his desire. As soon as his jaw opens to get what he wants, issue the "Take It" command. He will then associate this with securing a reward or treat. Now that he is playing with the toy, offer him another that is exactly the same. He will want both, causing him to drop the first toy to grab the second identical toy. Immediately when he releases the first toy, issue the command "Drop It." As he opens his mouth to take hold of the second toy, give the command "Take It." Repeat this command every day until he knows what to do. It's fun for him, but essential for you, as it means you will be able to take away anything your dog grabs that he shouldn't.

7. "No"

To stop unwanted behavior it is important to teach your OES the "No" command. First, put your Bobtail on a leash. Have two dog treats at hand. Place one dog treat on the ground and keep the other hidden in your leash-free hand. While your Bobtail is on a leash, slowly walk toward it. The second he tries to grab the treat issue the command "No." At the same time, pull your dog slightly against you using the leash. As he comes toward you and looks at you, give him the treat from your free hand and say "Yes" and give him lots of love and affection. Repeat the command over and over every day, and he will eventually get the idea.

8. "Leave It"

Teach your OES to leave unwanted items on the ground. For this command, keep a treat in both hands. Place one hand close to your Bobtail's face. He will smell it and lick your hand, and when he does, issue the command "Leave It." He will most likely bark to tell you he wants it, but after a little while will lose interest. The moment he does, give him the treat in the other closed hand. Repeat until immediately upon hearing "Leave It," he stops trying to get the first treat. When he tries for the second treat, give it to him along with lots of praise. This command is a tricky one to master, so you will need to do it every day.

9. "Crate" or "Bed"

Put your dog on his leash. Hold the leash in one hand and a treat in the other. Using the leash, guide the dog by moving the treat in the direction you want him to go and toward his crate, bed, or otherwise. The moment he gets in or on the correct place, issue the appropriate command, be it "Crate" or "Bed," and reward him with the treat. Repeat the exercise 3-4 times until he knows what is wanted of him. When you want him released from the crate or bed, grab the leash and say "Okay." Teach your Bobtail to respond to this command, and you can take control of bedtimes or whenever you need him safe and secure.

10. "Out"

Teach your OES to drop things from his mouth. Let your dog mouth one of his most treasured toys. Grab the toy and, keeping it close against your body, gently pull it toward you. At first, your dog will resist but eventually he will release the toy to you. At that moment, offer him the toy back and repeat the process. Once he loses interest and doesn't want the toy anymore, give the command "Out." For the best results, you will need to practice this every day.

11. "Wait"

Teach your Bobtail self-control by learning the "Wait" command. Walk your Bobtail toward the closed front door. Command him to "Sit." With your fingers, point upward, presenting him the palm of your hand and issue the command "Wait." As your dog waits, slowly open the door. As he moves toward it, close it. Doing this will let him know he must wait before crossing the threshold. You will need to do this every day, several times, until when you open the door entirely, your OES remains sitting, awaiting your command. When you are ready for him to walk, tell him "Okay" and reward him with a treat. This command is excellent for anyone who lives on a busy street.

12. "Okay"

The "Okay" command follows on from "Wait." Adopt an appropriate, encouraging tone and facial expression and tell your Bobtail it is free to walk on. It's a very versatile command to teach your dog. It teaches your Bobtail not to run free in public places, or into heavy traffic areas.

Once your dog is proficient with these commands at home, you can begin practicing them in a variety of more challenging locations.

Hand Signal Commands

All of the commands mentioned in this chapter so far are verbal. However, there is another option available when training your dog, and that is hand signal commands.

This form of training will help to improve your communication with your dog. Also, as your dog grows into his senior years, he may well lose some degree of hearing, and this is when you will both be happy you took the time and effort in the early days.

For this method to be successful, you will need first to teach your Bobtail to look at you continually. It is important that he hears the verbal command and sees the corresponding hand signal.

This form of training will take a lot of patience as your dog may not immediately respond. In the beginning, therefore, your Bobtail will need facial cues along with hand commands.

When your Bobtail understands the basics you can gradually phase out verbal and facial signals altogether.

Hand Signal Command Advice

- Keep hand signals simple.
- In the beginning, reward positive behavior with treats and praise. Gradually phase this out when he understands and is responding to the training.

Photo Courtesy
of Jewls Grossi

If your Bobtail already knows the basics, as in sit, stay, down, and heel, it's relatively plain sailing, but you will need to commit to some form of training daily.

Here, are 5 basic commands:

1. **Sit:** One Hand Palm Up: Very often, this widely used command is the first one that your dog will learn. Hold the palm of your hand at chest level, and so its facing the sky. In an upward motion, move your hand. In the beginning, combine this with the verbal "Sit" command.

2. **Stay:** Open Hand Palm Forward: Use verbal and hand signals for this command. Walk backward with the palm of your hand at chest level and facing outward. Your pet needs to remain where he is until asked to come.

3. **Lie Down:** Finger Pointing Down: Hold your finger pointed up to your chest and perform a sweeping diagonal motion downward. Hold a dog treat in your hand, and your Bobtail's nose should follow the direction.

4. **Come:** Hand Held Diagonally Across the Chest: Begin by placing your hand open at your side. Diagonally bring it to the opposite shoulder.

5. **Watch Me:** With One Finger Point to Eye: This is a vital first step. Your dog must learn to watch your hand signal, so whenever he looks directly at you, reward him with a treat.

Respect Training: Positive and Negative Consequences

Respect training equates to a balanced philosophy of canine training. Quite simply, it means using positive and negative consequences for your dog's good and bad behavior.

It aims to reinforce the idea that positive consequences encourage us to repeat good behavior, while negative consequences have the opposite effect.

This ethos relates as well to animals as it does to humans. For instance, when a puppy in a litter plays too roughly with his mother or siblings, he will be corrected with a growl. This teaches him to play more gently next time.

So when you are training your Old English Sheepdog and he reacts positively, reward him with toys, games, attention, praise, and dog treats.

On the flip side, when you need to correct the dog's bad behavior, correct him with your tone of voice, body language, by stopping the game, or returning him to the leash. What correction doesn't mean is physical or extreme verbal abuse. Remember, you are trying to correct your dog, not scare him and make him fearful.

It comes down to cause and effect. Your Bobtail will begin to make good choices because a) He wants a treat or attention, or b) He doesn't want to be corrected. Either way, he will begin to respect you, and do as he is told both willingly and enthusiastically.

Photo Courtesy of Cathy Nowack

Dog Training Tools: Clickers, Treats, and More

Regardless of which method you choose to use to train your OES, there are several supplemental tools that can aid the process.

Clickers

Thanks to their effectiveness and small price tag, clickers are arguably one of the most popular and commonly used tools for dog training. A clicker is a small, simple device that makes a clear, you guessed it, clicking sound. Clickers are used alongside positive reinforcement training. When the dog performs the desired act or behavior, the trainer uses the clicker to mark the moment before giving a reward, such as praise or a food treat. Doing so helps the dog to clearly understand exactly which behavior has earned him the reward.

Treats

Dogs are incredibly food-driven animals, which comes in very handy when training. Treats should ideally be blueberry-sized and not too hard. Speak with your vet or pet shop for advice on which treats will complement your OES's diet.

Target Stick

Target sticks are used more when teaching agility tricks, but can also be used to help your dog learn to walk nicely on a leash or go to a specific place like his bed or into the car trunk. Target sticks most often comprise an extendable handle with a ball at the end, on which you can spread a tasty treat such as peanut butter. The basic principle is to get your OES to be interested in the ball on the stick and touch it – this is where the tasty treat comes in! Once you have achieved this, you can begin to teach your dog to follow the stick.

Long Line

Consider investing in a long line while transitioning your dog from being on a leash to off-leash during walks outside the home. Longline leashes can extend to 15 feet or even up to 30 feet.

Harness

When it comes to training your Bobtail to walk nicely on leash, a harness can be more comfortable for both him and you. The harness makes sure the dog's neck is not being pulled too much, and it gives you more control over where he walks. There also special no-pull harnesses on the market specifically for leash training. The leash attachment is on the front of the harness on the chest rather than on the back between the shoulder blades. When the dog tugs, the leash causes tension across the chest that naturally slows him down without restricting his front legs.

Portable Dog Mat

Training sessions can be tiring, especially for small puppy attention spans! If you hold your training sessions out of the house, a portable dog mat is a great item to have with you so your dog can take a well-earned rest between repetitions. Look for a mat that is foldable, easily washable, and large enough for your Bobtail to lie down on comfortably.

Professional Dog Classes

Does the thought of obedience training your dog fill you with dread, and are you wondering if your Bobtail needs professional dog classes? Ask yourself if you're looking for a class specializing in certain behaviors or for a regular advanced commands class.

Seeking professional help for any dog-related training problem is not a fail. In fact, it can reap amazing rewards for you and your Old English Sheepdog. When it comes to dog training, it's better late than never.

Choosing where to take your Bobtail for classes can be overwhelming. There is a wide range of different types of training classes for dogs. Once you start your online research, you will discover lots of instructors with a whole host of different qualifications and membership affiliations.

For instance, in the UK, there is the Association of Pet Dog Trainers (APDT), while in the US you could check out the Certification Council for Professional Dog Trainers. You can also find out more from the American Society of Animal Behavior.

The best advice is to find a trainer accredited to an organization that has a set code of practice, a membership assessment system, and, very importantly, insurance.

Once you have found a class that you like the sound of, the next thing to do is ask to observe a class – without taking your Bobtail along. See if you like the instructors, helpers, and even the other participants – human and canine!

A professional instructor will welcome the opportunity to show-case his skills.

There are lots of things to look out for that can help you make a con-sidered decision as to whether a particular class is the one for you and your Bobtail.

These include:

- Paying close attention to the behavior of other dogs in the class. Are they anxious or scared? Are there too many other dogs in the class?

- Does the trainer use the negative and positive consequence method of training? Discount any classes that teach by fear or pain techniques.

- Is there a good instructor to dog ratio? As a general guide, for every 8 puppies, one trainer and one helper is a good number. Too many participants and it's difficult for the dogs to understand what is expected of them.

- Making sure that the class is calm with no shouting at either the dogs or their owners!

- Looking to see if the class is made up of all sizes of dogs. *When Charlie first attended a class, all his classmates were toy or small size breeds!*

- Making sure you like the style of training. For instance, is the instructor forcing dogs to participate causing them to become agitated, or are the dogs wagging their tails quite happily?

Finally, if you have the opportunity either before or after the class, ask some of the other dog owners how they have found the course and if it has reached their expectations.

CHAPTER 9
Breed-Specific Exercise Essentials

Your Dog's Exercise Needs

With the correct socialization level, your Old English Sheepdog will be confident, kind, and protective, with a stable and well-balanced temperament. However, he is likely to become strong-willed, destructive, noisy, and unhappy without the right level of human or animal interaction and company.

The inheritance of temperament is less easy to predict and is also shaped by how you raise your puppy and your dedication to initial and ongoing training.

Photo Courtesy
of Chris & Sarah Boak

Photo Courtesy
of Skyler Jokiel

While you will encounter unwanted behavior in dogs of all breeds, there is a small number of undesirable OES breed-specific traits you will need to look out for. These relate primarily to physical and mental stimulation or the lack of it.

An Old English Sheepdog needs space to run and romp. These dogs are a high-energy, intelligent breed. While they don't need to run for miles, they must have constant mental stimulation to avoid becoming bored. Boredom in adult dogs, as with puppies, can lead to unwanted behaviors such as stubbornness, excessive barking, whining, and destructive chewing.

To combat these issues you must have a clear understanding of your Old English Sheepdog's needs and then guide him along the correct path.

The best way to stimulate your Bobtail physically and mentally is through daily walks and fun exercises, both indoors and out.

Walks

Your adult Old English Sheepdog will thrive on no less than 60-90 minutes of daily exercise. Exercise produces endorphins and can help normalize your Old English Sheepdog's mood, improve brain function, and increase confidence.

As an energetic breed, your Bobtail needs to not only release pent-up energy, but also stimulate his mind with new sights, sounds, and smells.

Although, you will soon discover that your Bobtail's high stamina levels mean he can keep going indefinitely, the duration of your daily walk is dependent entirely on your lifestyle. Aim for one to two or more walks per day, depending on your schedule.

Remember, you are ideally aiming for a good workout rather than a gentle stroll around the block. This level of exercise is suitable for adult dogs around two to six years of age. A young dog under two is still in the growing stage, while a senior dog age seven and up will need its level of activity to decrease.

As dogs are creatures of routine, try to schedule daily walks around the same time each day. Avoid skipping daily walks in favor of an extended weekend hike. Your OES will thrive on consistency.

Photo Courtesy of Dave Paoletti

Photo Courtesy
of Helen Woods & Ian Pointon

Increasing Intensity

If you find yourself short of time, you can increase the intensity of your Bobtail's exercise by adding resistance to the walk.

You can do this using a weighted dog vest, which can help your dog let off steam, reduce stress, and increase cardiovascular fitness. Studies show that using a weighted dog vest can help support your dog physically and mentally. Weighted dog vests have a close-fitting design, which means your Bobtail's natural balance will not be compromised.

Additional benefits of weighted dog vests include:

- A vest will help your OES to push hard and, as a result, build muscle and tone, helping to prevent obesity.

- Increasing your Bobtail's strength can result in increased agility and stability.

- When time is short, a weighted vest will help your dog achieve a good workout, making him less inclined toward boredom related unwanted behavior. Wearing a weighted dog vest can reduce your Bobtail's stress levels.

More Information on Weighted Vests

When used correctly, a weighted dog vest can help you and your dog enjoy high-impact walks together. Consider the following points to ensure your Bobtail remains safe and comfortable:

- Check with your veterinarian on the suitability of purchasing a weighted dog vest for your OES.
- The vest must add a maximum of 10 percent of your dog's weight. Any more weight and you could overwork your Bobtail.
- Weighted vests are not suitable for dogs under two years of age. At this stage, your Old English Sheepdog is still growing and developing. As such, he is not yet ready for the additional stress on either muscles of joints.
- Refrain from using a weighted dog vest in hot weather as it may cause your OES to overheat.
- It is essential to purchase the correct size of vest for your dog. You can find information on this via the manufacturer or store from which you wish to buy the vest.

If you would prefer not to add resistance to daily walks, consider walking uphill or on different and more challenging surfaces such as sand.

Indoor Fun and Games to Challenge Body and Mind

"We use soccer balls for physical and mental exercise. If two people will play soccer with an OES this gives the OES a chance to physically run after the ball and mentally figure out where the ball is going next."

ANNETTE P SHORE
Carolina Shores

If exercising your OES outdoors is not always an option, you will need to get a little creative and look toward the great indoors! Here are several of the best, inexpensive indoor exercise ideas for your OES, all of which are stimulating for your Bobtail's body and mind.

Doggy Dates: Keep your Bobtail entertained by inviting a canine companion around for a play date. Give the doggy duo a few toys to play with and let the fun begin. One word of caution, things may get a little boisterous, so first remove any valuable or fragile items.

Fetch: Although you would ideally play this game in the yard or garden, if you have sufficient space in your home or garage, it's a great way to keep your OES active. To avoid any damage, throw your dog's favorite soft toy for a short distance, and instead of watching him chase after it, race with him.

Hide and Seek: The great thing about this indoor game is the whole family can join in the fun. A person needs to hide, and then call the dog by his name. When the dog discovers the person hiding, reward him with a healthy treat. Not only will your Bobtail get lots of exercise with this game, but it also provides a great bonding opportunity for other members of the family.

Obstacle Course:
Challenge your OES both physically and mentally. All you need are some old cushions, blankets, and sheets along with a couple of chairs and maybe a hula hoop. Make a tunnel for your Bobtail to run through or create small obstacles for him to jump over, and when he does well, reward him with lots of praise and a treat.

Scavenger Hunt: Here, your OES will have the opportunity to use his canine instincts. Encourage him to hunt for treats by scattering them throughout a room. Your dog will need to use his sense of smell for this exercise, so start by placing the first snack in an easy-to-find place. Once he gets the idea, you can be more innovative in selecting the hiding places; doing this will give his brain a workout too!

Tug of War: All you need for this fun game is a short length of rope or piece of cloth. Provided you have already established a trust relationship with your dog it's a great exercise to help your OES learn self-control. Trust is vital in this instance, as tug of war can promote aggressive behavior in some dogs. The same goes for puppies; while some pups enjoy playing this game, others may become aggressive. If this happens, choose another activity.

Treadmill Exercise: If you already own a treadmill, then why not use it as a way to help your Bobtail exercise indoors? Pop your dog on the treadmill, set the machine on the lowest speed setting, and let him get used to walking slowly before progressing to a higher speed. Reward him with healthy treats while he is using

OES IN FILM
Krypto the Superdog

Krypto the Superdog is a Warner Brothers animated series that follows Krypto the dog on his secret super-heroic adventures. Among the cast of characters is Drooly, an Old English Sheepdog voiced by Ty Olsson. Drooly's superpower is his drool, which he can use in various ways, including grabbing objects or as a projectile.

*Photo Courtesy
of Michele Hirata*

the machine. Doing this will keep him motivated to continue. When your Bobtail is happy with the speed, increase the level of difficulty to give him a good workout. If this is an indoor exercise he enjoys, you can always consider purchasing a dog-specific treadmill. These tend to be smaller and are therefore space-saving. Treadmill exercise must be supervised at all times, so always give your undivided attention to your Old English Sheepdog when choosing this activity.

Off-Leash Dog Parks: Indoor and Out

Are you considering exercising your Bobtail at either an indoor or outdoor off-leash dog park? If yes, then you must ensure that you, your dog, and the other dogs you meet at the park will be safe. Your OES will need to be well-trained, sociable, and have no guarding issues.

Off-Leash Dog Park Success

An untrained, off-leash dog can cause a whole heap of trouble. So before you set off for your choice of dog park, follow some basic steps, and prepare your OES for off-leash success.

1. Assess your Bobtail's on-leash behavior. An overactive, on-leash dog that whines, lunges, pulls, or barks when encountering other dogs will need some work. Ideally, when coming into contact with other animals, your OES should not jump up but instead calmly sniff.

2. Introduce your Bobtail to other on-leash dogs. If the other dog is aggressive or acts up, step in and take control. Position your OES behind you and guide him away from the situation. Never get in the middle of the dogs as you may get bitten. Doing this allows your dog to respect that you are in total control of the situation, resulting in your Bobtail relying on you to deal with any dog park issues rather than trying to deal with them himself.

3. Practice letting your Bobtail off the leash at home. If you have followed the command training advice in Chapter 8 of this book, your dog will sit and stay as instructed. Next, calmly move him outside. If possible, progress from your home to a secure fenced-in area such as a tennis court and practice, practice, practice!

4. When you can trust your Bobtail will return when called, move on to an unfenced park. Remain focused and give your dog your undivided attention. Turn cell phones off and don't allow your Bobtail to run wild. Practice the commands you have taught your dog.

*Photo Courtesy
of Stacie Bryant*

5. Before you arrive at the park, walk your dog around for 12-15 minutes. Your Old English Sheepdog must be calm before entering the park.

Indoor Dog Park Fun

If you don't have sufficient space to exercise your Bobtail indoors, you may want to look for an indoor dog park. These are off-leash, indoor dog parks where you and your OES can meet and socialize with other like-minded pet owners and their dogs, rain or shine. You will likely find staff on hand to control the free-running canine crowd, but don't expect a doggy daycare service. You must stay on the premises, look after your dog, and clean up any mess he makes. Each dog park will have its own method of making sure you and your dog are safe, and many have a vetting process before they allow you to join.

Rules and regulations will vary from park to park, but here are three pretty standard points.

1. You will need proof of up-to-date vaccinations and flea treatments. You may also need copies of your Old English Sheepdog's veterinary records or a letter from the practice.

2. The dog park may be adult-only, so before you join, check whether or not children are welcome at your park of choice.

3. Be aware that taking treats and toys to an indoor park is a no-no. Because dogs in enclosed areas may become possessive, wait until you leave the premises before rewarding your Bobtail.

The Great Outdoors

Your role at an outdoor dog park is vital. You will need to pay attention to your dog at all times and be able to assess and react to situations. You must accept full responsibility for your Bobtail's behavior.

A few factors can help you to choose an outdoor dog park that is right for you and your Bobtail.

First, check out the design of the park. Double gates work best, and preferably there should be two or three separate entrances. This option avoids dogs congregating, which can lead to increased arousal or even aggression.

Try and choose a large, unusually shaped park with either a lake or pond that your dog will find interesting. Hills and trees are great, too, as they shield dogs and can prevent them from bumping into one another. If there are no trees, look for man-made structures where timid dogs can hide.

When you are happy with your choice, make sure your visit to the dog park is a positive one. To do this:

- Check out which entrance you are going to use to avoid any "dog gangs."

Photo Courtesy of Ellen Reiser

- Pay close attention to your Bobtail's behavior, and interrupt his play if you feel he is too rambunctious.

- Move around the dog park. Do this so your dog keeps his focus on you and not other dogs. Don't be distracted by chatting with other dog owners. Keep your attention on your OES at all times.

- Remove your OES from the park if he is either being bullied or bullying others.

- When your Bobtail wants to leave the park, respect his wishes. Never let a scared dog remain somewhere he is uncomfortable in the hope that a situation will improve.

- Leave toys and treats for after play and when you have left the park.

Post-Park Playtime

Immediately once you both leave the park, reward and praise your OES, and head for home. Move your dog to a quiet place and give him some water. If you are traveling by car, just as you did on arrival, settle your dog down by walking him calmly, on a leash, for 12-15 minutes.

Overexercising and Overheating: Symptoms and Solutions

While it is vital to give your Old English Sheepdog sufficient exercise, it is also crucial to understand when you are overdoing his physical activity level. Overexertion can lead to muscle, tendon, and joint injury. A dog can also become overheated, leading to collapse, so you must learn more about potential overexercise problems and their solutions.

Signs that your dog may be overexercised may include:

Symptoms	Solutions
Overexercise	
• Exhaustion and taking a long time to recover after exercise. • Sleeping or resting more than is usual. • Excessive panting during or after exercise. • Extreme thirst. • Unusual lagging behind when it's time go. • Lameness, limping, or reluctance to continue or complete exercise. • Stiffness, sore muscles, confusion and/or lack of focus and attention.	• Reduce the amount and level of exercise for 2-3 days. • Massage your Bobtail to help loosen muscles and joints. • Soothe sore muscles using a heating pad. • Seek veterinary advice if symptoms don't improve, deteriorate, or are extreme
Overheating	
• Excessive whining, fidgeting, or confusion. • A tongue that is scooped at the tip and hangs out of the right side of the mouth accompanied by panting. • Red, dry gums and tongue. • Sluggish gait. • Breathing or gasping, foaming at the mouth, or thickened saliva. • Vomiting, diarrhea, or seizures. • Loss of skin elasticity. Dehydration can set in very quickly. To check for dehydration, grab the skin on the back of your Old English Sheepdog's neck and stretch it. It will return to its natural position very slowly if your dog is dehydrated.	• If your Bobtail is vomiting, has diarrhea, or is having a seizure call your veterinarian immediately. You must get your dog treatment as soon as possible. • If your OES is dehydrated, he will need a veterinarian to administer IV fluids. It is vital that if you see signs of this happening, you stop exercise at once and allow your OES to cool down. • Take your Bobtail indoors or move him into a shaded area. Your dog will need small amounts of water only. Prevent your OES from drinking too much water at once. • Using a cold, wet towel, cool the dog's front and back paws, belly, groin area, and under armpits. You must do this slowly as cooling down too quickly can cause your Bobtail to go into shock. For the same reason, do not cover your dog with a towel.

CHAPTER 10
Advanced Training Aids

Brain Training Interactive Toys

Exercise is not just about allowing your OES to burn off all that pent-up energy. A stimulated mind makes your Bobtail a happy dog, too. So, add some tasks to your exercise plan that will give your dog a job to do or present a mental challenge.

Photo Courtesy of Mike Leopando

Photo Courtesy
of Jan and Dale Wilkerson
Photo by Melanie Rene Photography

Five Reasons Why Your Dog Needs Interactive Toys

➤ They promote exercise

➤ Interactive toys stimulate the mind

➤ They help entertain your dog when you are busy

➤ Some toys cans help your dog maintain a healthy weight

➤ Mentally stimulating toys can control unwanted behavior by preventing your dog from becoming bored

Here, you will find some of the best brain training toys to flex your Old English Sheepdog's mental muscles and beat Bobtail boredom.

Treat Balls and Food Puzzle Toys

Add your Bobtail's favorite treats to a food dispensing ball or puzzle toy and sit back while he figures out how to get the snack. There are lots of these types of toys on the market. You will find that some toys present more of a challenge than others and most are made of rubber or plastic and are dishwasher-friendly. They consist of chambers that release treats when your OES rolls, paws, or nudges the toy. They come in lots of different colors and sizes.

This type of toy is ideal for helping your Bobtail to improve his concentration and memory skills. However, it is best to supervise your OES as he may become impatient and destroy the toy to get to the treat quicker.

Homemade Treat Toys

My brother's OES Charlie demolished indestructible toys in a matter of days rather than weeks! We came across two DIY brain-training, treat puzzle toy recipes. The first outlasted many, many others. It consists of a PVC pipe with holes in which you can hide your Bobtail's favorite snacks.

Try out the following instructions if you are looking to entertain your Bobtail on a budget.

Photo Courtesy of Pearl Yang

Photo Courtesy
of Skyler Jokiel

Directions:
1. Choose a selection of PVC piping and a variety of end pieces. Tees, end caps, and right-angle bends all work well.
2. Using a saw, cut the piping to your preferred length, approximately 10-12" long, but this will depend on the size of your dog. You will need to make a clean, smooth cut.
3. Put the end pieces on the piping.
4. With an electric drill, make some holes in the piping and ends. These need to be random and spaced out. The holes must be large enough to house kibble-size treats, and big enough to release the goodies, albeit with a little effort from your OES.
5. The two pieces on the right have large openings on the ends where you can smear peanut butter to prevent any kibble escaping. It will also take your Bobtail time to lick the butter out. Remember, when choosing peanut butter, it must be xylitol-free.

The second set of instructions is even easier and is perfect in hot weather.
Directions:
1. Fill a freezer-safe plastic bowl with water.
2. Pop a few chew toys along with some whole fresh carrots into the water.
3. Transfer to the freezer until frozen.

Photo Courtesy of Scarlett Brophy

4. Remove from the freezer, turn the bowl upside down, and remove the ice dome from the bowl.

5. Place the flat side of the ice facing downward on a grassy surface and watch your Bobtail lick his way to a treat.

Electronic Toys

These types of toys stimulate a dog's mind and gain his attention via lighting and sound effects. They are also a useful way to introduce your dog to sounds and sights he may or may not come across outdoors.

Ball Launchers

Most ball launchers operate using counter-rotating wheels. They squeeze the balls, which are then under pressure. This pressure forces the balls into a tube, which leads to an opening. All you have to do is feed tennis balls into a hopper. The hopper then shoots the ball out for the dog to catch or chase. It is easy for the dog to operate, so your Bobtail can play with the toy quite happily on his own. These kinds of toys can be useful, but should not replace playtime with you and your family.

Snuffle Mats

These are generally made of fleece strips of cloth that are woven through a heavy-duty back and tied. These create hiding spaces on the mat's surface. The spaces get filled with treats that your Bobtail can then have fun finding. This toy relies heavily on your dog's sense of smell.

Frisbees

Many OES owners, including my brother, say that a Frisbee is one of the best toys for physically and mentally stimulating their dogs. One of Frisbees' major selling points is that they don't bounce or change directions. This design means that your Bobtail won't have to swerve to chase the toy and is therefore at less risk of injury. You will need to choose a Frisbee that is durable and large enough for your dog.

Photo Courtesy of Gabrielle Rubin

Choosing the Right Toy

While on the subject of suitable brain training and interactive toys, here are some tips to help you choose the right one:

Size: It is essential to select the appropriate size toy for your OES. Toys that are too small for a dog's mouth can become a choking hazard, whereas a toy that is too large may be frustrating. Check the manufacturer's directions to help you choose the ideal toy for your beloved Bobtail.

Durability: Your dog is strong, and as such, you will need to select a durable toy. When choosing a toy, take your Bobtail's chewing habits along with the material of the toy into consideration before making an expensive purchase.

Safety: If your OES is allergy-prone, make a full inspection of the toy before purchasing. Avoid toys that have sharp edges or pieces that your Bobtail could bite off easily.

Suitability: The toy(s) you choose should be fun. Your choice should complement your Old English Sheepdog's taste and personality, so select a toy that he will find exciting and stimulating.

Keep in mind when choosing an interactive toy that it is an investment. Not only can it give your OES lots of fun, but it will also help to stimulate his brain and aid his overall development.

Photo Courtesy of Bob Hairgrove

High-Energy Classes and Activities

The benefits of dog classes and activities are two-fold. First, your Bobtail will get lots of exercise, and second, he will get to socialize with other dogs. Unlike indoor or outdoor dog parks, he will have the opportunity to do both in a more controlled and organized environment.

Old English Sheepdogs have high levels of stamina and are energetic, so search for classes and activities that will help your dog burn up a lot of energy in a short time. These could include indoor agility classes, high-intensity games, or even water sports.

OES IN THE WHITE HOUSE
Tiny

Franklin D. Roosevelt served as the 32nd president of the United States from 1933 to 1945. He was gifted an Old English Sheepdog named Tiny Tre on April 20, 1933, by Mrs. Helen Roesler. Roosevelt later gifted Tiny to Admiral Cary T. Grayson, a personal friend.

Canine classes and activities will help keep your Old English Sheepdog's muscles strong and their minds healthy.

Agility Classes

Don't be fooled into thinking that just because your OES likes to clown around, he isn't super smart and versatile. With the correct training, your Bobtail can excel at many sports, and dog agility classes are at the top of the list. Here, you direct your Bobtail through a preset obstacle course.

Your Old English Sheepdog must complete the course within a set time. Obstacles can include tire jumps, tunnels, seesaws, and tables, where the dog has to pause for a set amount of time. Your Bobtail must race around the course in the fastest time while taking instructions via your cues and body language.

Herding

Old English Sheepdogs are a herding breed, so they enjoy practicing their instincts whenever they have the opportunity, regardless of whether they are outdoors or not! Search online or ask your veterinarian for any information relating to herding classes.

These classes allow your Bobtail to learn from a professional in a controlled environment. Some carry out a herding test, whereby your Bobtail enters a small arena with well-behaved sheep. The trainer will observe and evaluate your dog's behavior and reaction to the sheep. The trainer will then come up with a plan for your OES to progress.

Photo Courtesy
of Cheryl Herbert

The American Kennel Club (AKC) runs a Herding Program offering tests and trials. It is offered in a non-competitive pass or fail format. There are three tests covering Instinct, Herding, and Pre-Trial. During a test, your OES must show his ability to move and control livestock. If your Bobtail enjoys herding, he can then move on to Herding Trails, which are competitive.

Swimming

Not all dogs love to swim. While some want nothing more than to join you in the pool, others are less enthusiastic when it comes to water. The best way to find out if your Bobtail is a water baby is to introduce him to the water slowly. If he isn't a water dog, then don't force him.

Dock Diving

If your OES does take like a duck to water, then dock diving might be a suitable activity for him to enjoy. Here, you throw your Bobtail's favorite toy into a pool while he waits on the dock. When you tell him to, the dog runs the length of the dock and throws himself off the end into the water to retrieve his toy.

The goal is to make the longest jump possible, which can range from two feet for beginners to 30-40 feet for more experienced dogs. One word of caution: expect to get wet!

Dog Driving or Weight Pulling

This controversial activity is the canine equivalent of a tractor pull. Dog driving or weight pulling is best suited for large breeds. A dog is tethered to a wheeled cart via a special harness. He must then use his body strength to pull heavy loads.

A typical cart is between 25 and 45 pounds, plus your Bobtail's body weight. The ideal ratio for pulling over long distances and your dog's body weight is 3:1. Check with your veterinarian before embarking on this activity.

Boating

If you're a boat fan, then why leave your Old English Sheepdog behind? Instead, follow these tips and enjoy some quality time together on the water.

- Check that the marina or park is dog-friendly.

- Prepare a first aid kit. You can include canine-specific anti-seasickness medication. Your veterinary will advise you on the best medicines to buy.

- Before going onboard, take your Old English Sheepdog on a walk for 10-15 minutes. Doing this will help your dog to calm down and also give him the opportunity to relieve himself. Take some absorbent pads along with you for the boat trip, just in case.

- Even if your Bobtail is a good swimmer, get him a well-fitting lifejacket or vest. A lifejacket will give your dog buoyancy and help him to float. In the unlikely event that your OES ends up in the cold water, neoprene models will also help to keep him warm. A fleece vest can also help your wet dog dry and stay warm.

- When you board, either carry your Bobtail onto the boat or, if he is too heavy, use a ramp. Embarking and disembarking must always be controlled and planned. If it isn't, your dog may attempt to jump.

- Fill your pockets with lots of dog treats. Positive reinforcement via treats can help to keep your OES under control, something that is especially important when you are busy baiting your line or dropping anchor.

- On the subject of bait, don't leave it lying around on deck. Your OES will find the smell of live worms very appealing. The same goes for any fish you may catch.

- Take a collapsible water bowl along with lots of fresh, clean water to last your Bobtail for the whole trip.

- If you are confident your OES won't dive into the blue, then allow him off the leash. The majority of adult dogs won't jump off a moving boat. Watch out, though, your Bobtail may decide to take a quick dip when the boat isn't moving!

- Remove any hooks, lines, or ropes to prevent your Bobtail from getting caught up and injuring himself.

- To prevent heatstroke, ensure that your OES has a shaded area.

- Lay either carpet or non-slip deck mats in the cockpit. These can prevent your Bobtail's big paws from missing their footing on slippery floors.

- Be prepared to head for home if things get choppy. Dogs get seasick too, and you don't want one horrible boating experience to put your Bobtail off for good.

Whether you enjoy recreational sailing or fishing from a boat, next time you take to the water, why not invite your canine companion along with you?

Getting Fit with Your Dog

Whether you are hoping to beat the bulge or stay in shape, there are plenty of fun ways to incorporate exercise into both you and your Bobtail's routine. Not only will you gain a super enthusiastic and fluffy workout buddy, but you'll be able to make the best use of limited free time by meeting both of your exercise needs in a single session.

Walking and running are not the only types of exercise that you and your OES can do together. From body workouts to yoga, there are lots of fun options available to your both.

To make the most out of these shared activities, your Bobtail will need to be calm and well-trained. Basic obedience is crucial—at a minimum, your OES needs to be 100 percent reliable with the heel, come, and leave it commands.

You can start small with this sample workout.

- Get moving with a 2- 3-minute walk
- Do 10 push-ups on the ground while your dog is in a sitting position
- Next, walk for 30 seconds followed by a 10-second sprint, then another 30-second walk
- 30-second plank with your dog laying down beside you
- 20-30 walking lunges with your dog at heel
- Repeat the exercise 3-5 times

The Downward Dog

Dog yoga is more popular than you may think. It isn't just about the poses and positions; it's about your Bobtail reading your energy and remaining calm. Old English Sheepdogs are intelligent and intuitive; they can easily identify and sense our emotional state via our breathing, tone of voice, and body language.

Dog yoga or doga, as it's sometimes called, is beneficial for calming hyperactive dogs. It is also a perfect exercise for obese or injured dogs. Many yoga poses mimic the way in which animals stretch, which enables your OES to quickly get the hang of this new activity.

Practicing yoga together can help you to form a closer bond with your Bobtail as well as providing a whole host of other benefits too.

It can:

- Improve your OES's circulation
- Aid relaxation and provide stress relief
- Be an effective behavioral therapy
- Soothe hyperactive or nervous dogs
- Help to develop impulse control

Although not as high energy as some other activities, over time and with patience, yoga is a way of exercising that you and your Bobtail can share.

Photo Courtesy of Nick Poling

Where to Begin

You have two options. The first is to find a class made up of other humans and dogs. The second is to practice at home.

Search for suitable classes online. If you can't find any, don't despair. Why not call your local studios and ask if they would be prepared to run a dog yoga class for like-minded people? Speak with your veterinarian too. Maybe he or she knows of other dog owners who would be interested in getting together with you and your dog and organizing dog yoga sessions in a local park.

If you prefer the comfort and peace of your own home and would prefer to embark on this new activity at home, all you need is your Bobtail, a yoga mat, and a quiet space where you will be uninterrupted.

Irrespective of your yoga experience, remember to go at your Bobtail's pace. Take your time, be patient, and be aware of your dog's physical limitations when it comes to certain poses.

Get on Your Bike

Only have 20 minutes to spare and a Bobtail buzzing with energy? Get on your bike!

Bike runs are a great way to cover a lot of ground in a shorter amount of time and are as simple as they sound. Hop on your bike, and with your Bobtail on a long, secure lead or running free next to you, set off!

Biking together with your pet is a great way to let him use up all that energy. Plus, he will get to set the pace without you lagging behind on foot slowing him down!

To begin with, make a few slow practice runs in a quiet, traffic-free area. Before you increase your speed, you need to ensure that your OES can run alongside you in a straight line without getting too close to the wheels, which could harm him.

Remember, you are pedaling to keep up with your dog's pace, not the other way round. If your pet is struggling to run fast enough to meet your speed, he could overexert or injure himself, and the experience will not be a positive one.

Bike runs are safest and most successful with dogs already trained to walk well on a leash or to heel. This is because trained dogs are more likely to stay close to the cyclist's side and not run ahead or in front.

CHAPTER 11
Traveling with Your Old English Sheepdog

Hit the Road: What to Take and How to Stay Safe

Whether it's a visit to the veterinarian, a walk on the beach, or a family vacation, regardless of your OES's age, the time will come when you need to hit the road.

Car travel, like a lot of other things, is something that it's best to get your Bobtail used to from an early age. Start as early as possible, gradually, and with short trips. At the end of the journey, reward your dog with his favorite treats; this will help him to have a positive association with the car.

As he gets used to traveling by car, take him on longer trips. Remember, though, to stop at least at two-hour intervals. Your Bobtail will need this time to have a drink of water and go to the bathroom.

Photo Courtesy of Tammie Hansman

Photo Courtesy of Gigi Rahman

You should never leave your OES alone in the car. However, in an emergency, make sure it's only for a short period and leave a window open.

To guarantee his and your safety, never leave your Bobtail free in the car. Not only might he distract you, but if you need to brake unexpectedly, he could suffer a serious injury.

Where in the Car Is the Safest Place for Your Dog?

Get your Bobtail used to being in a transport crate. For best results, get your dog used to this from the puppy or young adult stage.

Position the crate so that it can't move and is stable. You can do this using straps. Where you locate the crate will depend on the make and model of your vehicle.

There are a few options of crates and accessories to choose from, and these include:

- **Single and Double Door Folding Metal Dog Crates**

  These metal or wire crates are available in various dimensions to accommodate all sizes of dogs. Portable crates are lockable for added security. The double door option is a great feature as it offers ease of access. It's foldable, and the lightweight design means that it can be installed and collapsed in no time at all, making it space-saving and practical.

- **Trunk Grid and Separation Nets**

  One of the most convenient and safe ways to transport a large dog is in a vehicle with a trunk that opens into the car. Transporting your Bobtail in the trunk will keep him safe, and a purpose-built barrier will prevent him from jumping into the passenger side of the vehicle.

- **Heavy-Duty Barriers**

  Heavy-duty barriers are adjustable to fit a number of different makes and models of SUVs and cars. The barriers are generally constructed from steel and wire with a smooth surface designed to prevent your vehicle from being damaged or scratched. They are easy to install and remove and will keep you, your passengers, and your dog safe.

- **Mesh Barriers**

  This type of barrier is made from a durable, mesh material and is designed to be secured quickly and easily via adjustable straps and a support rod. Many feature storage pouches for leashes, toys, and poop bags. This barrier is intended as a deterrent. It will not prevent determined Bobtails from breaking free, meaning it is suitable only for well-trained and obedient dogs.

- **Net Barriers**

  Net barriers made from elastic mesh are a visible deterrent. They are meant to dissuade pets that are sitting on the back seat of the vehicle from disturbing the driver. The barriers are adjustable and flexible and can stretch to cover the space between the driver of the car and passenger. They often feature hooks to attach to headrests and the base of the seat. Again, these barriers are only suitable for dogs used to road travel and that are well-behaved and obedient.

- **Waterproof Trunk and/or Seat Covers**

  Prevent damage to, or dirt from getting on, the trunk or seats of your vehicle with a waterproof, wipe-clean cover. Many feature buckle straps for headrests and built-in Velcro openings for seatbelts. Available in all shapes, sizes, and colors to suit your vehicle. Seat covers are ideal for owners who need to transport their Bobtail in the back seat of their car.

Photo Courtesy
of Michelle Villalobos

- **Folding Dog Car Ramps**
  Help your Bobtail get in and out of high vehicles with a folding car ramp. If possible, choose a ramp with a removable, washable mat that is soft to protect paws and vehicle interiors. Many offer pressure-activated grip to ensure your Bobtail can confidently grip the mat's surface.
- **Dog Seat Belts**
  Dog seat belts are safety harnesses featuring a loop for seat belts to click through. They are designed for your Bobtail to sit comfortably upright or lie down while restrained. They can prevent your dog from jumping out of the car window.

Photo Courtesy of Mel Roo

Sundries

Whenever you travel with your Bobtail, depending on the length of the journey, make sure you have an adequate supply of pet sundries.

Useful items include wet wipes, poop bags, pee pads, chew toys, bottled water, a blanket, treats, and a collapsible water bowl. For longer journeys, prepare a first aid kit. Have extra collars, leashes, and tags with an up-to-date cell phone number.

Prepare a list of nearby veterinarians and take copies of your Bobtail's vaccination record and any medications. If your Old English Sheepdog is prone to car sickness, leave a one-hour gap between food and a road trip. Your veterinarian can advise you on suitable motion sickness medication.

OES IN FILM
Muppet Dog

If you grew up watching *Sesame Street*, you might remember a big fluffy Muppet named Barkley. The orange and white dog was modeled to look like an Old English Sheepdog and was introduced to *Sesame Street* in the tenth season. Unlike other characters on the show, Barkley doesn't speak, but communicates through barking and is often seen with Big Bird.

Before You Set Off

One final word of advice: not all dogs love the open road, and some can get very nervous or overexcited at the prospect of a road trip. Whenever possible, 24 hours before travel, exercise, exercise, and exercise! A tired Bobtail will be a lot easier to cope with on a long car journey!

Take to the Sky: Air Travel

Air travel with your dog is a complicated affair. Not only do you have to worry about additional costs and individual airline policies, but also about your pet's safety and comfort.

These worries can be amplified when traveling with large-breed dogs, as most airlines prohibit large dogs from traveling in the cabin with their owners.

The majority of airlines classify dogs weighing more than 22 pounds as "large."

It is likely impossible to find an airline that will allow your OES to travel in the cabin. However, some allow large-breed dogs aged from 8-10 weeks and above to travel in the cargo hold or checked-in baggage compartment.

With air travel rules continually changing, you will need to contact your chosen airline for clarification before planning to travel with your OES. Depending on the airline and your final destination, you may need a pet passport and for your dog to be microchipped.

If you are lucky enough to take to the skies with your Bobtail, follow these pre-travel flying tips.

- Make an appointment with your veterinarian and check that your OES is healthy, and all his vaccinations are up to date and per the airline's terms and conditions.

Having flown many times myself with rescue dogs traveling to their new homes, a good tip is to get your pet used to his travel carrier at home a few weeks before flying.

- Source and purchase a suitable pet carrier. As a guide, your Bobtail must be able to stand, turn, and lie down while crated. The carrier must be durable, leak-proof, and have a padded base with ventilation on opposite sides. The airline will have rules regarding size and material, etc. Label the crate with your name, home address, destination, and cell phone/email details. On all sides of the carrier, paste "This Way Up" and "Live Animal" stickers.

- Allow 4-6 hours in between feeding and flying your dog. Doing this can help to avoid travel sickness.

- Most airlines do not permit owners to tranquilize their dogs unless they have documentation from a veterinarian. This is because sedating your Bobtail can result in him vomiting during the flight, having a fatal reaction due to air pressure changes, or losing his balance.

- Check if the airline will allow you to pack absorbent pads, toys, and blankets in the crate. Again this varies from airline to airline. If your Old English Sheepdog is allowed a blanket, consider giving him one of his unwashed favorites. The familiar scent will help to calm and reassure him.

When you are ready to fly, arrive at the airport two to three hours before needed along with your Bobtail and his documents.

Some organizations specialize in arranging flights for large dogs. You can research this option online.

Canine Cruising

While some shipping lines ban dogs on cruises, they do make exceptions for service animals. Requirements vary, so you will need to contact the relevant company before taking a canine companion onboard.

When it comes to recreational pet-friendly cruise ships, there is only one, Cunard's *Queen Mary 2.*

On certain sailings between New York and Southampton, you can cruise with your Bobtail. You will need to contact the shipping line for a full schedule of sailing times.

While you're enjoying the luxury facilities on board, when not exercising, your OES will find himself confined to canine quarters in an onboard kennel rather than sharing a cabin with you. The good news is, though, he will receive a welcome-aboard gift!

Photo Courtesy
of Aly Mui

Photo Courtesy of Scarlett Brophy

While on the high seas, specific crew members led by the Kennel Master will feed, walk, and clean up after your dog. He will also enjoy treats and toys. Playtime is organized, and there is an off-leash dog area as well as an indoor play space. You can visit your Bobtail at set times of the day. Be aware; there is no veterinarian onboard.

The ship can provide food for your OES, and the kennel attendant can cater to any special requirements on request.

There are 24 kennels on board (12 on the upper deck for small dogs and 12 on the lower deck). Only two lower kennels are available for larger-size dogs, so you will need to reserve your OES's passage 12-24 months in advance. Depending on the size of your Old English Sheepdog, it may be necessary to book multi-kennel accommodations.

Requirements for travel may be subject to change.

For eastbound crossing from New York to Southampton

- Your Bobtail must have a microchip.

- Have received a rabies vaccine 21 days or more before boarding.

- Hold an official Veterinary Certificate within ten days of the cruise.

- Be treated against heartworm disease one to five days before joining the vessel.

For westbound crossings from Southampton to New York

- Hold an official Veterinary Certificate within 30 days prior to entry into New York.

- Have received a rabies vaccine. You will need to check for the most recent vaccine from the United States CDC.

Pet owners holding an EU pet passport are not permitted to have the passport updated by a Canadian or US veterinarian. It must only be updated by an EU or UK veterinarian.

For more information and current details of luxury cruising with your Old English Sheepdog, contact the Cunard line.

Finding Dog-Friendly Accommodations

If you intend to travel with your Old English Sheepdog, one of your biggest concerns is likely finding dog-friendly accommodations.

Before you embark on your great adventure, the first thing to consider is your dog's strengths and weaknesses. Your Old English Sheepdog's limitations will have a considerable bearing on your choice and type of accommodation.

If your Bobtail likes the sound of his voice, a hotel is most likely not the right choice. Excess barking may also end up with the hotel asking you and your dog to leave.

Bobtails that bark may be a lot more suited to a pet-friendly Airbnb-style property, bed-and-breakfast, motel, or out of the way cabin.

So what can you do to prevent spoiling other guests' enjoyment?

- First of all, when you make a reservation, ask for a ground floor room. Your OES is heavy, and it will eliminate the worry of noise from boisterous paws on the ceiling to the room below.

- If available and funds allow, upgrade to a suite. The benefit of having a living room as well as a bedroom means your OES will be further away from any activity going on outside the room.

- Ask about the accommodation's pet policy. Some may not allow pets to be left alone, while others may have time limitations.

- Ask the hotel, too, if they have a list of local pet sitters they could call to stay with your Bobtail while you are out.

- Avoid leaving your OES alone in the room. Remember, everything will be new to him, from the smell to the sounds.

- Opt for takeout or room service, and if you are visiting family and friends and it's not possible to take your Bobtail with you, ask them to visit you in the hotel instead.

- Pack a couple of old towels and sheets to take with you to protect any soft furnishings.

- Take a pet hair removal brush with you for any soft furnishings.

- Groom your OES before arrival.

- Before you leave your room, take time to establish the room as your new home. Leave a jacket on the back of a chair, or spray your perfume or aftershave around the room. This way, your OES will realize that you are coming back.

- Take your Bobtail's blanket or bed to the hotel with you. Your dog will be a lot calmer, surrounded by familiar things. Also, if you intend to travel with a crate, when you leave the room, consider covering the crate with a blanket. Hopefully, this will encourage your dog to sleep while you are out.

- Pack any puzzles or toys your Bobtail likes for him to amuse himself with while you are out.

- If leaving your OES for a short period is unavoidable, then here are a few simple steps to help you avoid any problems.

    - Tire him out before you settle him down.

    - Before leaving the room, help your OES relax with soft music and leave it playing to help mask any outside noises that may trigger barking.

    - Report to the front desk that you are leaving your Bobtail alone, give them your cell phone number, and ask them to notify you of any issues.

Photo Courtesy of Dylan Kinsella

Leaving Your Dog in Good Hands: Boarding Kennel versus Pet Sitter

If coming to terms with leaving your Old English Sheepdog in a third party's care is giving you sleepless nights, then approach it from a different angle. A kennel is a hotel, and all the other guests are dogs.

If that still doesn't sit right with you, there is the pet sitting option. A pet sitter, either a professional, a dog-loving friend, or a member of your extended family, stays in your home while you are away. Alternatively, the pet sitter visits your property to attend to your Bobtail's daily needs.

Boarding Kennels

If your OES is a puppy or young dog, boarding kennels may be the better option for both of you. You may be a lot happier knowing that your Bobtail's needs will be attended to on a round-the-clock basis. You can arrange for your dog to have special attention, such as long walks, grooming, and fun days out. All of which are ideal for a boisterous and rambunctious OES. Better yet, boarding will eliminate any destructive behavior in the home.

If you have more than one dog, they should be able to share a kennel and keep each other company.

It is a lot easier to familiarize your OES with boarding if you do this from an early age. Kennels can be a traumatic experience for any breed of dog. Your Bobtail will suddenly find himself alone in a new place with lots of different sights, sounds, and smells.

If you are planning a long trip in the future, then consider boarding your OES at your chosen kennel for one or two days a few weeks before an extended stay. Doing this will get him used to the idea of kennels and reassure him that you are coming back for him.

Before you make your reservation:
- Ask other dog owners, your breeder, pet shops, and your veterinarian for boarding kennel recommendations. Check out their websites and look for relevant review sites and social media.
- If finding a boarding kennel with a recognized accreditation is important to you, ask your veterinarian what you should be looking out for.
- Ask the boarding kennel of your choice for its experience with large breed dogs.
- Ask to visit the kennels and facilities. Check out the facilities, including sleeping and exercise areas. Are areas clean and well-tended? Boarding kennels will have some odor, but the smell shouldn't be overpowering.

- If the weather is cold, ask about heating and if it is hot, inquire about air conditioning. Either of these options may incur an additional charge.
- Does the boarding kennel offer any additional services? These could include beach or forest walks or pre-pick-up grooming.
- Ask about veterinarian care in case of an emergency.
- Check if there is an option to provide your own dog food.
- Request a feeding and exercise schedule.
- Check the kennel's requirements regarding vaccinations.
- Find out if the kennel staff is available 24/7. If not, make a note of the times that you can call.

On arrival at the boarding kennel:

- Give the kennels one of your Bobtail's favorite blankets and chew toys. The familiar scent will comfort him and help him settle down in the new environment.
- Give the kennel details of your veterinarian and any required documentation, including vaccination certificates, special medication, etc.
- Advise your vet of the name of the kennel and the duration of your OES's stay.
- Email and write down your contact details, journey details, and alternative contact in case of an emergency.
- Ask the boarding kennel for an update of your dog's progress every couple of days.

Pet Sitters

If you have a senior OES, he may feel less stressed at home, surrounded by familiar sights and smells. Your Bobtail will also be able to follow his routine of food, exercise, play, and sleep time. He will receive one on one love and attention from the same person while at the same time not coming into contact with other dogs who may have unwanted parasites or, at worst, illnesses. For this option to be a success, your Old English Sheepdog should be obedient and well socialized around friends and strangers.

Before you book a pet sitter:

- Make sure you have chosen the best person for the dog. You can do this via personal recommendations or by asking your veterinarian.
- Check out relevant review sites and social media to discover what other dog owners are saying.

- If the pet sitter is a stranger to you, ask for references, and follow up on them.
- A professional sitter should also be insured and bonded. Ask to see any necessary paperwork and make a copy.
- Before booking, invite the prospective pet sitter to your house to meet your Bobtail. Take them on a walk with you and see how your dog reacts outside of the house. It also gives the sitter an idea of how your Bobtail performs on the leash.

After booking a pet sitter:
- Provide the sitter with a comprehensive list of your Bobtail's feeding and exercise needs.
- Provide the sitter with information regarding your OES's favorite puzzles and toys.
- Show your pet sitter how to groom your dog.
- Before you leave, give the sitter your destination contact details and an itinerary of where you are day by day. Also, add an alternative contact in case it's not possible to get hold of you.
- Write down the full contact details of your veterinarian for the sitter and determine how they would transport your OES to the vet in case of an emergency.
- Contact your veterinarian surgery and give them the name of the pet sitter and your written authority to treat your Old English Sheepdog in an emergency.
- Make sure your OES has an ID tag on his collar and that the details are up-to-date.
- Insist that the sitter gives you a report of your dog's daily progress along with phone photos every two days or so.

Your choice should depend on the particular needs and personality of your OES. Either way, peace of mind that your Bobtail is safe and happy is paramount.

CHAPTER 12
Pride and Groom

"It's best to start brushing them the day you get them. They need to get use to different styles of brushes from the very beginning because their life will be full of brushing and grooming."

ANNETTE P SHORE
Carolina Shores

Photo Courtesy
of Jennifer Payne

Caring for Your Dog's Shaggy Coat: Brush, Bath, and Beyond

Old English Sheepdogs may have a care-free, fun-loving nature, but when it comes to grooming, they are arguably one of the most high-maintenance and demanding dog breeds. That trademark soft shaggy coat will soon turn into an uncomfortable matted mess without regular intervention.

You can introduce your puppy to the world of bathing, nail clipping, and trimming from 12 weeks of age. Grooming your OES is not just about keeping up appearances. A severely tangled coat may lead to mobility issues. What's more, regular grooming will help you spot any irregularities or issues that may require a vet check. These irregularities could include sores, growths, or rashes on your dog's skin, which could go unnoticed when covered by layers of fluff.

Now that we have established why it is so essential to maintain a regular coat grooming routine, let's delve deeper into precisely what that routine should involve.

Brushing

Long shaggy coats are prone to mats and tangles, especially if your dog loves spending time outdoors. Removing the dirt and debris that creates these mats and tangles is one of the most important reasons to brush your OES. However, it's not the only benefit.

Regular brushing also:
- Distributes natural body oils, helping to keep skin and coat moisturized
- Keeps your dog's coat looking fluffy and full
- Promotes proper circulation
- Helps minimize shedding

Prevention is better than cure, and for that reason, I recommend brushing daily. Brushing daily will help you to easily remove small pieces of dirt and debris before they create larger mats and tangles. It may seem like a big commitment, but dedicating just ten minutes per day to brushing out your Bobtail's coat will prevent a long, painful session of detangling at the end of the week.

As the saying goes, "A workman is nothing without his tools." Choosing the right brushes for the job will make the process easier and more comfortable for you and your Bobtail.

Below are some of the best Bobtail-friendly brushes and products that will make your life a lot easier when it comes to grooming:

Pin Brush: Pin brushes work well on dogs with coarse, long coats. With long, stainless steel pins, these brushes can penetrate deep into your OES's thick coat, removing dirt and debris from both the top layer and the under-coat. When purchasing a pin brush, look for types with rounded tips rather than ball tips; this will help prevent the pins from becoming tangled in the fur.

Grooming Comb: After giving your pet the once-over with a pin brush, it is a good idea to follow up with a grooming comb. These types of combs typically have stainless steel teeth that separate the hairs and work to prevent mats. They are an ideal finishing tool and will help to give your OES that sought-after fluffy appearance. Consider buying a larger grooming comb for the body and a small comb to work in areas such as around the face, ears,

Photo Courtesy of Chrissy Barry

and backs of legs. Look for combs with a comfortable grip handle; this will help you prevent it from flying out of your hand.

Detangling Spray: Brushing out a coat while dry can cause damage. Using a detangling spray will not only make it easier to brush out tangles but will also help to condition and moisture the coat, to prevent future matting. There are many detangling sprays on the market; look for one that uses natural ingredients and no harsh perfumes. If in doubt, ask your veterinarian or trusted pet store for their recommendation.

Brushing Steps

1. Work one area at a time, such as the head and shoulder area. Spritz with your chosen detangling spray. Don't forget to ensure to protect your OES's eyes while spraying. Take your pin brush and gently begin brushing through the coat, with the grain, in short strokes.

2. Separate the hair with your fingers to ensure you are reaching deep into the coat.

3. Use your small grooming comb to brush around delicate areas such as the ears and paws. Make sure to do both the front and back of the paws. Also, lift the ears and brush gently underneath.

4. Repeat, working in sections until your Bobtail is brushed all over.

Bath

It is a good idea to bathe your OES every six to eight weeks, or even sooner if you have been on an outdoor adventure! Bathing such an energetic breed may seem daunting, but good preparation can make the process smoother. Follow these steps for bath time success:

1. Always brush your Bobtail to remove any mats or tangles before bathing. It may seem tempting to skip this step, but when your dog's coat tangles and mats get wet, they tighten and fuse, making them twice as difficult to remove.

2. Have plenty of towels ready and make sure to place some on the floor. Splashing is inevitable, even with a well-trained Bobtail.

3. Place a rubber mat in the base of the bath to prevent slipping.

4. Have your chosen shampoo ready. Your shampoo should ideally be for long-haired dogs with coarse coats. Your trusted pet store will be able to recommend a suitable product. Do not use products intended for humans.

5. Have a small flannel or washcloth ready.

6. If you do not have a handheld shower attachment, have ready a sizeable plastic mug so you can pour water over the dog. Turn on the showerhead and check the temperature before getting your OES into the

tub. Adjust the gauge so that the water temperature is neither too cold nor too hot. Run the water over the underside of your wrist to check that the temperature is suitable

7. Place your OES in the tub and do not remove his collar. If you don't have a second pair of helping hands, you may need to hold your OES's collar to prevent him from jumping out of the tub. Alternatively, you may wish to step inside the bath or shower along with him.

8. Using the handheld shower attachment or plastic mug, douse your dog all over with water until he is soaked completely.

9. Apply the recommended amount of shampoo to the coat and massage into a lather.

10. Rinse away the shampoo until no suds remain, and the water runs clear.

11. Soak the prepared washcloth and use it to gently clean around your dog's face and ears.

12. Using your hands, squeeze as much water out of the coat as possible.

13. Remove your OES from the bath and dry him off as much as possible using towels. Try to rub downward rather than ruffling up his fur to prevent matting. You can either finish drying with a hairdryer on a low heat and speed setting or allow your dog to dry naturally. While drying, do not let your pet to sit in any drafty area.

14. Once your Bobtail is fully dry, finish with a quick brush.

Beyond

Besides regular bathing and brushing, you should check your OES's paws, rear end, and privates for overgrown hair. Overgrown hair can be more serious than it sounds. For example, in the paw pads, overgrown hair can mat become painful, and in extreme cases, even cause lameness.

Every other week, I recommend using a small pair of nail scissors or specialized grooming scissors and checking the following areas:

Paws: The fur should be flush with the paw pad to allow your dog's paws to grip the ground and prevent slipping. Use a small grooming comb first to brush out the hair and then carefully trim the excess fur around and between each paw pad.

Rear End: To keep your dog hygienic and healthy, it is essential to ensure his rear end isn't covered with excess hair. He should be able to poop without any excess fur getting in the way. To begin, brush your OES thoroughly to remove any mats and tangles. Brush the fur flat over his read end. The fur at his rear end should cover his bottom area but not hang more than one inch below it. Trim this excess hair.

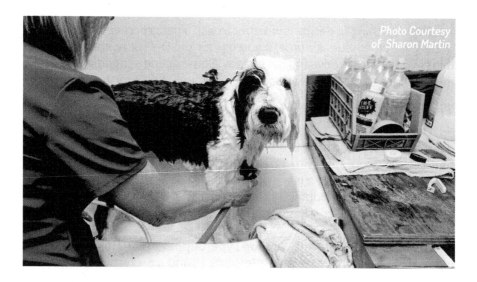

Photo Courtesy
of Sharon Martin

Private Areas: If the fur around your pet's private area is not regularly trimmed, when he pees, he will likely soak his fur. Not only can this cause him to smell unpleasant, but it also creates a breeding ground for bacteria, which increases the likelihood of infections. Using small scissors, trim any excess fur that could interfere with urine flow when your OES pees.

If you don't feel confident using scissors at home to trim your Bobtails excess fur in these delicate areas, it is best to take him to a professional groomer.

Nail Trimming and Maintenance

Generally, most dogs' nails wear down naturally thanks to regularly walking on hard surfaces such as concrete, paving stones, cobbles, asphalt, and tar, etc. This means there is no need to cut your Old English Sheepdogs nails if he regularly goes outside.

However, for a Bobtail that doesn't regularly walk on hard surfaces, his nails will grow and likely need trimming.

You will know when this happens because you will hear a tapping sound on some floor surfaces, or you will see your dog struggling to walk comfortably as he is forced to walk on his nails rather than his pads. Once your Bobtail's nails are beginning to protrude too far from the pads, it's time to clip his claws.

Your Bobtail's toenails consist of the nail and the pink-colored quick. This quick supplies blood to the nail and will bleed if cut. It is also very sensitive, so if this happens, it will cause pain to your OES.

The next thing to decide is whether to visit a pet groomer or veterinarian or deal with the issue at home. If you opt for the DIY route, there are a few things you need to know and have ready. Some online shopping or a visit to the pet store to buy the necessary equipment may be in order.

The Right Tools for the Job

Get your OES used to having his feet handled. Do this a few times every day leading up to the trim. Every time he remains calm and is happy for this to happen, reward him with a treat. Doing this will make a home trim a lot easier. It could take you a week or two for him to reach his comfort level.

To cut and trim a Bobtail's claws, you will need to select a dog nail clipper. There are a variety of different nail clippers on the market. The most common three are:

Professional Dog Nail, Scissor-Type Clippers (For Home Use): This type of clipper will have stainless steel blades and a protective safety top to

Photo Courtesy
of Pat and Kathryn Haran

help you avoid overcutting. It will cut cleanly and precisely. You will need to check the recommended weight for using this type of clipper as your Old English Sheepdog's nails will be thick and strong.

Guillotine Style Clippers: These trimmers have a stationary horseshoe-shaped hole. You place the nail into the ring. The cutting blade moves up and slices off the nail when you squeeze the trimmer's handles. You may find some types are neither strong enough nor large enough to accommodate a larger dog's nails.

Dog Nail Grinder: Another trimming option is a dog nail grinder (filing machine). Follow the same steps as you would when using a professional nail clipper. Be aware that with this type of device, there will be some vibration and noise.

When trimming nails in this way, on-hand snacks are super important. The best way to approach the task is to first to turn the machine on. Next, feed your OES a treat for 3-5 seconds. Turn the machine off so your dog learns that machine on equals a snack; machine off equals no snack. Continue with this method until your Bobtail's nails are the preferred length.

Nail Trimming at Home

If you have chosen a manual nail clipper, the next thing to do is proceed with the job in hand by following these simple steps:

1. Gather a light source, your nail trimmer, and a few food treats. Also, have some styptic powder just in case you make a mistake. This powder will help stem the blood flow.

2. Thoroughly clean your Bobtail's legs and paws.

3. Sit on the floor in a well-lit room with the door closed and no visual or audible distractions.

4. Your OES needs to sit or lie next to you.

5. Take one leg and using the light, locate the vein of the claw. It is vital not to cut the vein, so trim only a small amount of the nail. Proceed by slowly cutting the nail, end by end, stopping the moment you see a point in the middle. If you are having trouble finding the quick, apply a drop of baby oil to the nails. Doing this will help make them more transparent and therefore easier to see.

6. Reward your Bobtail as you progress to help him remain motivated.

7. Repeat the process until all his nails are sufficiently trimmed. Alternatively, if you can't do all the nails in one go, clip them one paw at a time, with breaks in between paws.

8. Use the same method for dewclaws (the curled back nail on the upper part of the paw).

Photo Courtesy of Merrilee Rush

Maintenance

If you neglect nail trimming and allow them to grow too long, you are opening your OES up to all sorts of problems, including hip, shoulder, and joint issues. So check your Bobtail's nail growth every 14-21 days.

Healthy Eyes, Teeth, and Ears

Caring for your Old English Sheepdog's grooming needs involves a lot more than keeping his shaggy coat looking good.

For any dog, including your Bobtail, making sure that eyes, teeth, and ears are well maintained and properly cared for is not only good for their appearance, but also for their health.

Your Old English Sheepdog's Eyes

Some breeds of dogs are more prone to eye issues than others and with that long fringe, your Old English Sheepdog's eye care routine should be top of your to-do list.

Below are two of the most common eye-related issues specific to the OES breed.

Tear Stains	**Problem:** It is not unusual for light-colored dogs to develop brown tear stains in the lower corner of the eye. They are common in breeds like the OES due to the amount of hair surrounding the eye.
	Solution: Using a canine-specific tear stain wet wipe, clean the tear stains. Alternatively, clean using a cloth dampened with a canine-specific eye rinse. If there is only tearing in one eye, the cause could be a blocked tear duct. If this is the case, make an appointment to see your veterinarian.
Eye Gunk	**Problem:** Eye gunk can form in the corner of your Bobtail's eye, making him susceptible to bacterial infections and other issues.
	Solution: Prevent eye gunk from causing a bacterial infection by regularly rinsing your Bobtail's eyes when mucous is visible.

How to Clean Your Bobtail's Eyes

Do's: Find a quiet room with no audible or visual distractions. Using a damp sponge or cloth, gently wipe the eye area to loosen and remove dirt and debris. Approach your Bobtail calmly, so as not to startle him.

Use dog-specific eye wipes and solutions only.

Don'ts: You must not wipe the eye itself. Never use shampoo or soap near your Bobtail's eyes as this causes irritation or, worse, will damage the eye(s).

Protecting Eyes

1. Before bathing your dog or using a flea-killing treatment, use a dropper to apply an ophthalmic gel for pets. This gel will prevent any chemicals from irritating your Bobtail's eyes. You can buy the gel online or from most pet stores. If you are unsure about using this product talk to your veterinarian.

2. Do not allow your OES to put his head out of a vehicle's window while driving. Preventing him from doing this will eliminate any dirt, debris, or dust particles from coming into contact with and irritating his eyes.

A Winning Smile

While Old English Sheepdogs are not prone to dental problems, your Bobtail's dental health is vital for his overall wellbeing, and therefore, it's not something you should ignore. Just like their owners, there are a number of oral diseases that your OES can suffer from, many of which can result in more serious problems later in life.

Brushing twice a week and an annual trip to your veterinarian is highly recommended if you are to keep your OES's teeth and gums in tip-top condition.

First, you will need to choose the correct type of toothbrush along with a canine-specific toothpaste made using dog-friendly ingredients. You can buy these from most good pet stores, online, or maybe from your veterinarian.

Tooth Brushing

Prevent dental disease and tooth decay with regular brushing. Brushing a dog's teeth is not the easiest thing to do, so you will need to persevere and start slowly. While your Bobtail will find brushing a strange sensation at first, with a little patience, he will soon get the hang of it!

To prevent gum disease, decay, plaque, and tartar build-up, invest in a good quality dog toothbrush.

There are many different types available, and these include:

Dual-Ended Toothbrush: A simple tool is often the best for the job. This style of brush features a large head on one end and a small end on the other. It can cater to dogs of all sizes and will break down plaque and food debris. Its bristles are soft and gentle, which makes it easy to use.

Finger Toothbrush: Some Bobtail owners may find it challenging to use a dual-ended toothbrush. In this case, the finger toothbrush could very well be the answer. The brush head is placed on the end of a finger, making it easy to move around your Bobtail's teeth and gums and get into difficult to reach areas. Bristles are soft, and some brands are available in different finger sizes. It is easy to clean and durable enough to last for two to three brushings.

Electric Toothbrush: If you are looking for a toothbrush to break down even the toughest tartar build-up, then an electric model is the answer. It works in the same way as its human counterpart, vibrating and working through tartar or plaque. Some models feature an LED light to allow you to view the inside of your Bobtail's mouth and identify any potential dental issues.

FUN FACT
Runner Up!

In 2013, a Colorado OES was the reserve best in show at the annual Westminster Kennel Club dog show. His registered name is Bugaboo's Picture Perfect, but his family calls him Swagger. The pup, who was only 22 months old at the time, was also named best of breed and best of group in 2013. His owners are Colton and Heather Madison. They own a local kennel in Colorado Springs that sheltered a number of displaced pets during the Waldo Canyon fire. The mayor presented Swagger with the Spirit of the Springs Award in 2013 in recognition of his award-winning accomplishments and his owners' charity.

*Photo Courtesy
of Jill Kelpin*

Toothbrush Stick: If your Bobtail is very reluctant to allow you to brush his teeth, then opt for a toothbrush stick. These are like a regular chew toy, but provide 360 degrees of cleaning power. The rubber stick is surrounded by bristles that will remove dirt and debris and freshen your Bobtail's breath. All you need to do is squeeze a pea-size amount of canine toothpaste into the hole on the top and allow your dog to do all the work as he chews. Dental chews can be a great option but be aware that some are high in fat and calories, so choose wisely.

Toothpaste

The first rule of brushing your dog's teeth is never to use human tooth-paste. Why? Because many human kinds of toothpaste are sweetened with xylitol. This artificial sweetener is toxic to dogs and can cause a drop in your Bobtail's blood sugar as well as liver damage. So keep your OES safe and always use canine-specific toothpaste.

Once you have all the tools you need, it's time to get brushing!

1. Choose a quiet time of day for brushing teeth in a calm, well-lit space where there are no distractions, visual, or audible.

2. Make sure your Bobtail is calm and comfortable.

3. Touch your dog's front, side, and back teeth both top and bottom gently with the brush. Give him lots of praise and encouragement for allowing you to do this.

4. Squeeze a pea-size amount of canine toothpaste onto your finger. Allow your OES to smell and lick the paste.

5. Add a small amount of toothpaste to the brush.

6. First, brush your Bobtail's top teeth. To do this, hold your dog's top lip up, and brush. Praise as you brush.

7. Gradually, progress from the front teeth to the back and side of the top set of teeth.

8. Next, begin to brush the bottom set of teeth. Hold down the bottom lip and brush the bottom teeth. Begin with those in the front of the mouth, gently working to the sides and back. If your dog is comfortable with the brushing, try to brush the inside of the bottom teeth too. Here is where plaque can build up, and it may be more difficult to brush. It may be something you have to build up to, over time.

After each step praise your Bobtail and reward him with a treat. Yes, this does on the surface seem counterproductive. However, once you have successfully mastered the art of teeth brushing, you can remove treats from the equation.

Clean Ears

It is recommended to check your Old English Sheepdog's ears regularly and clean as needed. Doing this will help to remove any build-up of grime and avoid the possibility of an ear infection.

How often you should do this is dependent on your Bobtail's everyday environment. For example, do you live in dusty, sandy, or muddy conditions? Is your OES running in long grass or densely wooded areas and at danger from ticks?

When it comes to ear cleaning, as with eye and teeth brushing, you must choose dog-specific solutions only. You can find these online at your local pet store, and in some cases, your veterinarian.

Once you have chosen the product, it's time to clean your Bobtail's ears.

To do this:
- Take your OES to a quiet place outdoors, free from audible or visible distractions.
- Make sure your dog is calm and preferably lying down.
- Place the dogs head in your lap.
- Pour the canine ear solution into the ear canal until it starts to overflow into your dog's ears. Avoid squeezing the container too hard as it may result in air pockets.
- Massage your Bobtail's ear gently at its base. Doing this will ensure the fluid works itself into the ear correctly. Stand well back, while your dog shakes his head. This vigorous shaking will remove any dirt, debris, mud, wax, or gunk; hence, why you need to do this outdoors!

- Repeat the process for the other ear.
- Gently wipe out and dry both ears using a soft, clean cloth. You must never use a Q-tip.

If your OES excessively scratches his ear, or you see a discharge dripping from the ear, redness or scabbing, or your Bobtail appears off-balance, he may be suffering from an ear infection and you'll need to make an appointment with your veterinarian.

You should also regularly check your Bobtail's ears for ticks.

Warning Signs of an Ear Infection Can Include:
- Ear Scratching
- Head-Shaking
- Rubbing Head on the Floor
- Redness, Scabbing, or Swelling
- Discharge or Foul-Smelling Odor from the Ear Area

How to Check your Bobtail's Ears for Ticks

When checking your Old English Sheepdog's ears for dirt and grime, also look for ticks. These eight-legged parasites will latch onto your OES and feed on his blood.

Ticks can transmit disease to humans so care must be taken when removing them from your dog. We will be further exploring tickborne diseases in Chapter 13 of this book.

Before you begin to remove any ticks from the ears, you will need:
- Disposable Gloves
- Tweezers
- A Ziplock Bag
- Permanent Marker Pen
- Isopropyl Alcohol

To examine and remove ticks follow this procedure:
1. Look deep into each ear.
2. If you discover any ticks, using your fingers and wearing disposable gloves, part the fur around the tick
3. With the tweezers, grasp the tick as close to the skin as you are able. Slowly pull the tick out of the skin.

4. Transfer the tick to the Ziplock bag. Seal and write the inspection date on the bag before placing it in the freezer. If your dog shows signs of sickness over the following months, your veterinarian will find this useful.

5. Dab alcohol on the site of the tick removal. While this won't kill any tick-carrying diseases, it will clean the area of bacteria.

You can follow this procedure for removing ticks from any part of your Bobtail's body.

Professional Grooming Options

"It is essential that you train them to lie on their side on a grooming table. This is easy when they are a puppy, not so much as adults! You should be able to touch all parts of their body and have them remain still. I use the command "head down". If the head is on the table so is the rest of the dog!"

DEA FREIHEIT
SnowDowne Old English Sheepdogs

Due to the extensive level of grooming Old English Sheepdogs require, many owners seek professional help. The best way to find a competent groomer for your OES is to carry out some online research, or ask your veterinarian along with other dog owners for suitable contacts and referrals.

It is not feasible to have your OES brushed daily by a professional, so it's one job you can't get out of! However, if you don't have a suitable bathroom for bathing your dog at home or are nervous trimming around sensitive areas, taking your pet to a trusted groomer is a great option.

A trained groomer will be able to take care of those tasks that require more skill and knowledge, such as plucking hairs from inside the ears, examining anal glands, and removing large mats.

Some owners are hesitant to make regular grooming appointments for reasons of cost. One thing to consider, though, is that during just one session, your groomer will likely use more than 15 tools. These tools include a sturdy grooming table, professional-grade clippers, multiple brushes, otic solution, skin and coat care products, nail trimmers, and a dog-suitable hair dryer. If you were to purchase all of these items to use at home, the total outlay would likely well exceed that of several appointments.

When it comes to grooming, each breed has its own specific needs, so try to ensure your chosen salon has experience with Old English Sheepdogs before booking an appointment.

Photo Courtesy
of John Oehler

Coat Clipping

Your Bobtail's coat is double-layered and consists of a weather-resistant fine and soft undercoat and a textured outer coat.

It is a common misconception that all long-haired dogs should be clipped down to the bone in summer to help keep them cool. In actuality, your Bobtail's long coat not only provides warmth in winter temperatures but also provides cooling shade in the summer heat. Clipping his coat too short could cause him to overheat more.

When clipping your OES to prepare for warmer weather, ensure you take him to a groomer with specific breed experience. An OES-experienced groomer will know to clip your dog and leave enough hair to provide shade and help your Bobtail maintain his body temperature.

Of course, you can choose to go it alone when it comes to clipping your OES, although it isn't something most Bobtail owners would recommend. The sheer amount of mess it will create is one reason. The second is that for clipping, you need top of the range, professional tools that you are unlikely to have access to at home. Due to an OES's coat's thickness, commercial-grade clippers will get worn down very quickly and may even get stuck in your pet's fur.

CHAPTER 13
Health Care

Veterinary Visits

Don't wait until your Old English Sheepdog is unwell to visit your chosen veterinarian.

Making an unscheduled visit to your veterinary practice for a friendly chat will ensure your Bobtail doesn't associate a trip to the vet with something he should fear.

Scheduled Check-Ups

In addition to casual drop-ins, regardless of whether your OES is in tip-top condition, it is crucial to schedule regular and annual veterinarian check-ups.

These check-ups will allow your veterinarian to identify subtle changes in your OES's overall physical and mental health. Regular visits are particularly important if your dog is senior or has specific health needs.

Like humans, as your Bobtail advances in age, he will suffer from more aches and pains. While this is no cause for concern, a check-up will enable your veterinarian to monitor your OES and identify any underlying health issues quickly.

Photo Courtesy
of Melissa Solis

Prevention Is Better than Cure

Veterinary appointments are the ideal time to discuss any problems causing concern. These could include lumps, bumps, or any swellings you may have noticed, along with changes in temperament.

It is also the perfect opportunity to discuss your Bobtail's food and water intake and activity levels.

In most cases, your veterinarian can help you manage many health problems with medication or simple lifestyle changes.

How Often Should Your Bobtail Visit Your Veterinarian?

How often you should schedule a check-up will depend very much on your Bobtail's age, development, and any concerns or issues you may have relating to his health; however, below is a general guideline.

Puppies – Birth to 12 months: Up to 16 weeks of age, you will need to visit the veterinarian for vaccination purposes every 3-4 weeks. Your vet should also examine your Bobtail at around 24 weeks to discuss future neutering, spaying, and microchipping.

Your veterinarian will also check that your puppy walks and stands correctly and is alert and bright.

Adults 1-7 Years: Depending on your Bobtail's general health, it is recommended that your dog visit the veterinarian once a year. During the first annual check-up, your vet will administer any necessary booster shots in accordance with state guidelines.

If you have any concerns regarding your OES's health, it is a sensible idea to take your dog's stool sample along with you.

Seniors 7 Years and Up: Aim to visit your veterinarian twice a year. These check-ups are vital for following up on any issues. If he feels it necessary, your veterinarian may carry out tests to check liver, kidney, and heart function as well as test hormone levels, blood, and urine.

A top to tail check-up with your veterinarian may include:
- Weighing your OES and monitoring his weight
- Making a full examination of your dog's joints, paws, and legs
- Monitoring your Bobtail's heart and lungs
- Checking your OES's reproductive organs and abdomen to highlight any irregularities such as tenderness to the touch, swellings, lumps, or excessive heat
- Examining your Bobtail's teeth and gums and advising on any necessary treatments or cleaning. It is usual to also check for tartar buildup, broken or decayed teeth, and excessive salivation

- Advising you on flea and tick prevention and providing you with information on how to avoid roundworm, tape, and lungworm
- Making a thorough check of your Bobtail's coat and skin to ensure that it's not overly dry or oily and that no dandruff is present
- Examining eyes for discharge, redness, or excessive tearing
- Checking ears for discharge, hair loss, or thickening
- Arranging any diagnostic screenings that may be necessary, including X-rays, blood tests, etc.
- Carrying out any necessary vaccinations and updating health cards or records
- Scanning your Bobtail's microchip to ensure it has not migrated, and is readable.

Photo Courtesy of Pearl Yang

Vaccinations and Neutering

Vaccinations for Your Bobtail

Vaccination can help prevent a number of pet illnesses. Many believe it is the most efficient way to enable your dog to live a long and healthy life. There are various vaccines available to prevent a number of diseases.

While vaccination has many benefits for your Bobtail, it is a procedure that can also carry risks. It is up to the owner to evaluate these pros and cons, alongside their dog's health and lifestyle.

Speak with your trusted veterinarian, who will talk you through all of the options available to help protect your Old English Sheepdog.

Vaccines Explained

Vaccines help to prepare your dog's immune system to fight off disease. They contain a small amount of the virus that they are trying to protect your dog against. They work by exposing your Bobtail's immune system to the virus so that it recognizes the virus.

When the vaccine is administered, the body's immune system is stimulated. If your Bobtail is then exposed to the actual disease, his immune system is ready to recognize the disease and fight it off or reduce its impact.

Your veterinarian will advise you on a vaccination schedule for your Old English Sheepdog. Timings will depend on the type of vaccine needed, your Bobtail's age, medical history, and lifestyle. Vaccinations may be a part of your Bobtail's scheduled check-up, but failing that, most veterinarians will send owners a reminder.

Possible Vaccination Side Effects

Stimulating your Bobtail's immune system can create unwanted symptoms. Most symptoms don't last very long, while some may need medical attention.

Signs to look out for needing veterinarian attention include:
- Fever
- Soreness, swelling, scabbing, hair loss, or pain around the injection site
- Loss of appetite
- Sluggishness and lethargy
- Vomiting or diarrhea
- Lameness
- Breathing difficulties
- Seizures

- Collapse
- Hives and/or facial swelling

There is only a small chance of your dog suffering from adverse side effects. However, it is a sensible idea to schedule a vaccination appointment at a time when you are at home with your Bobtail to monitor his reaction to any treatments.

If you suspect your Old English Sheepdog is having an adverse reaction to a vaccine, contact your vet at once.

Core and Non-Core Vaccinations

There are two types of vaccinations available to your Old English Sheepdog: core vaccines and non-core vaccines.

Core vaccines are considered essential for all pets based on their risk of exposure, disease severity, and transmission to humans. Non-core vaccines are administered depending on the dog's risk of exposure.

- Core Canine Vaccines

Distemper: This viral disease is often fatal. It affects the respiratory and gastrointestinal (GI) tracts and often the nervous system. Distemper causes serious illness, and, in some cases, the disease is fatal.

Photo Courtesy of Lauren McCall

Parainfluenza: A viral disease that affects the dog's respiratory system.

Parvovirus: This viral disease causes severe diarrhea and vomiting and is often fatal. It may be involved in the development of kennel cough.

Hepatitis/Adenovirus: The vaccination protects against Adenovirus types 1 and 2. Type 1 causes canine hepatitis. This viral disease affects the liver, along with other organ systems. Type 2 causes respiratory illness and may be involved in the development of kennel cough.

Rabies: This fatal viral disease attacks the nervous system and is contagious to humans. Each state has its laws governing the administration of the rabies vaccine. While some may require annual rabies vaccinations, for others, it's every three years. In the majority of states, rabies vaccination proof is mandatory.

- Non-Core Canine Vaccines

Bordetella: This bacterial infection can cause or contribute to kennel cough.

Coronavirus: This viral disease causes diarrhea. The risk of infection is not as great as other viral diseases.

Giardia: This vaccine can prevent shedding of cysts but not infection.

Leptospirosis: This bacterial disease can be fatal. It affects a number of systems, including the liver and kidneys. It is only a risk in specific geographical locations. Dogs that are exposed to stagnant water or the urine of wild animals are at greater risk. If your Bobtail is living in a rural environment or spends a lot of time outdoors, you may want to consider this vaccine.

Lyme disease: Ticks spread this bacterial disease. It can cause kidney disease, arthritis, and other issues.

Canine Influenza Virus (CVA): This virus causes flu-like symptoms and is highly contagious to other dogs they are in close contact with, for example, at a dog park. You may find that some grooming salons and boarding kennels require your Bobtail to have received this vaccine before entering their premises.

Discuss your dog's specific vaccination needs with your veterinarian.

Spaying and Neutering

Neutering is a form of sterilization for male dogs that is carried out under general anesthesia. In most cases, vets will suggest that your Bobtail is neutered or spayed between the age of four and nine months.

For female dogs, spaying involves the removal of ovaries and the uterus. For males, neutering means removing the testicles.

Here are some points you may want to consider before deciding on the procedure:

Spaying Your Female Bobtail

Pros:

- You may avoid some health issues. Without ovaries, there is no risk of ovarian cysts or cancer, and no uterus means no risk of uterine infections or cancer.
- Spaying a female dog before she reaches puberty will reduce the risk of mammary tumors developing.
- When a female has no desire to mate, her temperament will naturally become calmer.
- Spaying your female Bobtail will result in less mess caused by bloody discharge.
- You won't have to deal with the consequences of an unplanned pregnancy such as having to care for or find suitable homes for unwanted puppies.

Cons:

- One in five dogs reacts badly to anesthesia. As spaying requires anesthesia, the procedure can prove life-threatening in a small proportion of cases.
- Spaying may increase your Old English Sheepdog's chances of urinary tract infections and incontinence.

  Your Bobtail may become less active, and as a result, gain unwanted weight. The loss of sex hormones (estrogen and androgen) can cause your dog's metabolic rate to decrease, thus lowering energy levels. For this reason neutering and spaying is linked to weight gain or obesity.
- The operation is irreversible, so you will no longer be able to breed from your Old English Sheepdog.

Neutering Your Male Bobtail

Pros:

- Neutering a male dog can decrease his risk of prostate cancer.
- Neutered dogs tend to become calmer and less aggressive over time.
- Testicle removal will reduce your Bobtail's desire to spray and mark his territory, especially in the house.
- Neutering will reduce your Old English Sheepdog's urge to mate, mount other dogs, or leg-hump humans. It will also make him less likely to stray as he searches for his next mate.

- Your OES will not be able to impregnate female dogs resulting in unwanted puppies.

Cons:

- Your dog will require anesthesia, and this can cause a number of adverse or life-threatening complications.
- Positive changes in behavior cannot be guaranteed.
- Neutering your Bobtail can lead to incontinence.
- Your Bobtail may become less active, and as a result, gain unwanted weight. The loss of sex hormones (estrogen and androgen) can cause your dog's metabolic rate to decrease, thus lowering energy levels.
- Neutering can sometimes cause hypothyroidism (underactive thyroid gland) which can also result in weight gain.
- The operation is irreversible, so you will no longer be able to breed from your Old English Sheepdog.

If you have rescued a dog that is not already spayed or neutered, then this is something you may wish to consider and discuss with your veterinarian.

Flea, Tick, and Worm Treatments

Warning

Before we investigate the many forms of preventative flea and tick treatments available, note that some dog breeds are sensitive to certain pest prevention products. Studies reveal that over the last 20 years, many herding breeds of dogs are particularly susceptible to adverse drug-related reactions. Reactions can include skin burn, skin irritation, seizures, and death.

The reaction is caused mainly by a gene that is resistant to regular doses of the drug that renders it toxic to dogs that carry the gene. This gene is known as the multidrug resistance 1 gene (MRD1). It is an inherited condition. You can arrange with

OES IN FILM
The Shaggy Dog

The Shaggy Dog is a 1959 Walt Disney film about a boy who turns into an Old English Sheepdog and goes on a number of misadventures. The black-and-white film is based on a 1923 novel entitled *The Hound of Florence,* written by Felix Salten.

your veterinarian to have your Bobtail screened to establish whether or not he has the MDR1 gene.

Three drugs that may trigger an adverse reaction in a dog with the MDR1 gene and used in flea treatment medications are ivermectin, milbemycin, and selamectin. As a herding dog, the Old English Sheepdog is one of the affected breeds that may suffer from severe side effects when using some products. For this reason, you must talk to your veterinarian before purchasing or applying any flea products.

Parasites: Explained

Adult fleas are parasites that live on the neck, back, and underside of dogs and cats. The eggs, larvae, and pupae live off the host animal. Before they latch onto your Bobtail, they can be found in humid, moist, and shady areas. Fleas can thrive in the home, yard, and garden all year round.

Eight-legged parasites, ticks, bite your Old English Sheepdog and drink his blood. Although initially very small, when they attach themselves to your dog by burying their mouthparts in their skin, they can swell to the size of a large pea.

Fleas and ticks are small, which is why for a dog with a shaggy coat such as an Old English Sheepdog, regular grooming is a must.

You will need to check with your veterinarian before buying any form of over the counter flea or tick preventative medications. The different options available include oral medications, spot-on treatment (administered topically) and flea collars.

Photo Courtesy of Meghan Nikituk

Worms

There are five main types of worms that affect canines. These are heartworms, hookworms, roundworms, tapeworms, and whipworms.

1. **Heartworms:** Heartworm is a serious disease that results in severe lung disease, heart failure, other organ damage, and potentially death. The worms are spread through the bite of a mosquito.

2. **Hookworms:** These short, blood-sucking parasites with teeth strip nutrients from pups. Some dogs will experience extreme weight loss, dull and dry coat, coughing, or bloody diarrhea. For some puppies, severe hookworm infection can prove fatal

3. **Roundworms:** Two types of roundworms can affect dogs. They are Toxocara Canis and Toxascaris Leonine. Both types are long, white, and have a spaghetti-like appearance, and absorb valuable nutrients from the affected animal.

4. **Tapeworms:** As the name suggests, these worms are long and flat. Some tapeworms may be over six inches long. When your dog excretes these worms in their feces, they split into rice-like segments. They can cause vomiting, weight loss, and anal itching. Some tapeworms that infect dogs can cause serious diseases in humans too.

5. **Whipworms:** Whipworms have a thick anterior end and a long thin posterior end, resembling a whip. The thicker end embeds itself in the dog's intestinal wall. As the whipworms mature, it causes the host to suffer from discomfort and irritation. They are one of the most common canine intestinal parasites.

There are many ways that heartworm and intestinal parasites such as hookworm, roundworms, and tapeworms can come into contact with your Old English Sheepdog.

- From mother to puppy. An infected dog, when nursing, can pass hookworms and roundworms on to her pups.

- If your Bobtail likes to scavenge, he can catch worms from other infected animals. These can include birds, sheep, and rodents.

- Your Bobtail may contract worms by eating the feces of worm-infected animals.

- A dog can contract worms when self-grooming. If your OES swallows a roundworm egg on its coat, a new roundworm infection may develop. The same goes when swallowing fleas during grooming. Doing this can lead to a tapeworm infestation.

- Your Bobtail can contract heartworm from mosquito bites.

Ways to identify that your OES has contracted worms:
- Your Bobtail is rubbing or scratching his behind along the floor.
- Worms are visible in your Bobtail's vomit.
- Your dog's belly or stomach is unusually bloated.
- Worms or eggs are visible in your dog's rear end and surrounding fur.
- You can see worms or eggs in your Bobtail's feces.
- Bloody diarrhea is present.
- Changes in appetite. Your dog has an increased hunger but is losing weight.

Prevention and treatment of worms

To help prevent your dog from contracting worms, always pick up and effectively dispose of your Bobtail's feces as quickly as possible.

Talk to your veterinarian about the various worming treatments suitable for your Old English Sheepdog.

Your Bobtail will require one to three initial doses of the recommended worming treatment to kill the worms, followed by a dose to kill any new worms.

Natural ways to treat and prevent worms

Are you concerned about the side effects of conventional worming products? If so, there are some natural ways you may want to consider when treating worms.

Apple Cider Vinegar: This vinegar will increase the alkaline levels in your dog's intestines. Add ¼-1 teaspoon of apple cider vinegar to your dog's water bowl every day. Doing this will not only help eliminate worms but also improve your Bobtail's coat.

Carrots: Carrots are a source of vitamin A. When digested, coarsely chopped carrots scrape the dog's stomach walls, removing any mucus or parasites. Feed them as a tasty treat.

Coconut: Dried coconut is a vermifuge, serving to expel worms or other animal parasites from the intestines. Sprinkle 1 tablespoon of coconut over your Bobtail's food.

Raw Pumpkin Seeds: These seeds contain the amino acid cucurbitacin. This amino acid paralyzes the worms, efficiently eliminating them from the animal's intestine. Feed them to your Bobtail whole, as a treat, or ground into a fine powder sprinkled over their food. Feed your OES one teaspoon of seeds for every 10 lbs of body weight, twice daily.

Turmeric: This superfood is believed to boost the immune system. It boasts antibacterial, anti-inflammatory, and anti-fungal properties. It has four compounds that can help rid the body of worms, repair the intestine, and result in a healthier gut. Combine the turmeric with coconut oil to create a paste to feed to your OES.

These foods alone may not get rid of every worm infestation, so discuss these options with your veterinarian to assess their suitability and effectiveness.

Holistic Health Care

Many different holistic practices may benefit your dog when he isn't responding to traditional medicines and procedures. These alternatives can be used in conjunction with regular veterinary treatments to improve your Bobtail's overall health. For example, your OES may require a surgical procedure and also benefit from some form of holistic health care to ease pain and inflammation and speed up the healing process.

Your veterinarian may already be combining regular vet care with holistic therapy, so talk to him about alternative treatment methods.

From acupuncture to canine massage, here are just some of the holistic alternatives you may want to consider for your Old English Sheepdog.

Acupuncture

Acupuncture is a 5,000-year-old Chinese therapy. It works by inserting thin needles into the human or canine body. The needles placed in identified pressure points enhance blood circulation. The aim is to encourage your Bobtail's body to correct energy imbalances and begin to heal itself. Your OES may benefit from this treatment as acupuncture is believed to improve blood circulation, reduce pain and anxiety, and more. Consult with your veterinarian before using this form of therapy.

Aromatherapy

Calming scents can help an anxious dog. If your OES is anxious or stressed out by thunder, fireworks, or separation, an essential oil mister may be the solution. Don't forget, though, dogs have a heightened sense of smell, so you will need to talk to your veterinarian before going ahead with this method of treatment.

Dog Massage

Massage is not only relaxing, but it can also soothe sore muscles, improve oxygenation, blood flow, reduce pain, and ease your Bobtail's stress and anxiety levels. Many experts claim it also helps to remove toxins, decrease blood pressure, and aid digestion. Better still, most dogs seem to enjoy it! You can learn how to massage your OES yourself or ask your vet to recommend a trained animal massage therapist.

Magnetic Therapy

This therapy can help dogs suffering from joint problems. If your Bobtail has mobility issues, you could consider buying him a magnetic dog pad to lie

Photo Courtesy
of Jessica Foster

on. These have specifically placed magnets embedded in them, and studies show they can help increase mobility.

Soothing Sounds

Studies show that for humans, music affects the nervous and cardiovascular system. There is now further evidence that certain types of music can help to calm an anxious, stressed dog. Deborah Wells, an animal psychologist and behaviorist, studied how different types of music affect various dog breeds. Deborah discovered that dogs in a shelter environment, when subjected to music from Bach, Beethoven, Brahms, and Vivaldi, barked less and spent more time in a state of rest.

Veterinary Chiropractic Treatments

Using low force, veterinary chiropractors manipulate the animal's spine and bones to relieve muscular, skeletal, and joint problems. Consult your vet for advice, treatment availability, and options.

Common Health Problems

In most cases, an Old English Sheepdog's lifespan runs from 10-12 years, and although most live a happy and healthy life, others may have some inherited health issues.

Thankfully, these problems, if identified at a young age, can be treated. Common problems include:

Cataracts: Cloudy areas within the lens of the eye, cataracts will negatively affect your Bobtail's vision and, at worst, lead to total blindness.

Cataract symptoms include changes in eye color, pupil shape or size, cloudy gray or white pupils, rubbing or scratching of the eyes, watery eyes, unsure footing, and clumsiness. Senior dogs are more prone to cataracts, but they can appear at birth or early on in your Bobtail's life.

Deafness: There are over 30 large dog breeds susceptible to deafness. The level of deafness can be partial, complete, or affect one or both ears. Your veterinarian will carry out a non-invasive computerized test to identify the level of your Bobtail's deafness.

It's possible to perform the test from as young as six weeks old. It will cause no pain to your OES and will give you peace of mind that your dog's hearing is normal.

Hip Dysplasia: This hereditary disease affects large breed dogs. It is the most severe orthopedic disease. Here, the hip joint's ball and socket do not fit or develop correctly, causing them to rub and grind. It causes looseness and leads to an eventual erosion of the hip joint and arthritis.

Symptoms include decreased activity and range of motion, difficulty jumping, running, climbing stairs, reluctance to rise from a lying position, rear-end lameness, a bunny-hopping gait, shoulder muscle enlargement and loss of thigh muscle mass, pain, and stiffness. If identified early, diet modification, anti-inflammatory drugs, pain medication, herbal supplements, and physical therapy will go a long way towards decreasing the severity of hip dysplasia.

Your veterinarian can carry out a physical examination of your Bobtail if he suspects hip dysplasia. Still, you must lookout for any of these tell-tale signs yourself.

Hypothyroidism: This congenital condition results from a lowered production of thyroid gland hormones. To identify this condition, be aware of any unexplained weight gain, lethargy, recurring skin infections, and excess shedding. Treatments include diet modification, synthetic hormone medication, and herbal remedies. These treatments will resolve the majority of systems in a matter of three months.

Progressive Retinal Atrophy: This eye disease is an inherited disorder of the retina. It occurs in both eyes and is non-painful. Its clinical signs include dilated and glassy pupils. The good news is that if your veterinarian diagnoses this condition before your Bobtail loses his vision, antioxidant and nutritional supplements may help.

Gastric Torsion or Bloat

Gastric torsion, or "bloat" as it is commonly referred to, occurs in certain breeds of dogs, including Old English Sheepdogs, due to their deep and narrow chests.

Often large-breed dogs wolf down their food quickly, gulp air, and drink large quantities of water straight after eating, followed by strenuous exercise. All of these are factors that contribute to a dog experiencing bloat.

When a dog suffers from gastric torsion, the stomach twists on itself and fills with gas. This twisting action can result in the death of your Bobtail as it cuts off the blood supply to the stomach, and at times, the spleen.

Blood flow to the dog's heart will slow and the volume blood pumped through the heart decreases, leading to cardiac arrhythmias. Next, the stomach lining begins to die, and toxins will start to accumulate. Other organs, such as the liver and pancreas, for example, can also become damaged. Low blood pressure causes shock to set in, and in severe instances, the stomach may rupture.

The veterinarian will perform blood tests and X-rays to confirm the condition. Your Bobtail's condition may be such cause for concern that your vet may decide to start treatment before receiving the results.

To treat the shock, your veterinarian may administer intravenous fluids and steroids along with antibiotics and antiarrhythmics to treat an abnormal heartbeat. He will then, using a stomach tube, decompress your Bobtail's stomach and wash the stomach out to eliminate any accumulated gastric juices and foods.

In most cases, this treatment will not be enough, and surgery will need to be performed to straighten out the twisted stomach. This procedure is complicated and does not always have a positive outcome.

How to recognize gastric torsion

If your Bobtail is suffering from gastric torsion, he will demonstrate signs of abdominal distension, salivation, and retching. Your OES may become restless, weak, lethargic, depressed, have a rapid heart rate or appear anorexic.

Should you notice any of these symptoms or suspect your Bobtail of having bloat, you must contact your veterinarian or animal hospital at once.

Some dogs die within three days of experiencing a serious case of bloat.

Ways to help prevent gastric torsion

- Do not use an elevated food bowl
- Prevent your OES from exercising 60 minutes before and after a meal
- Serve your dog two meals a day rather than one large one
- Make sure your Bobtail has fresh water throughout the day
- Make mealtimes as stress-free as possible to help to slow down your Bobtail's eating

Can gastric torsion be prevented with surgery?

Gastropexy is a preventive operation that a veterinary surgeon can perform on your OES to prevent his stomach from twisting. The procedure involves stitching or tacking the stomach to the inside of the belly. Performed correctly, it has a 95-percent success rate.

There are three optimum times for your veterinarian to perform this preventive surgery.

1. When your Bobtail is under anesthesia for an alternative procedure such as spaying or neutering
2. At the discretion of you and your veterinarian
3. In the event of your OES undergoing surgery to treat gastric torsion, gastropexy is mandatory. Talk to your vet and ensure that this procedure will be carried out at the time of surgery. If it isn't, the condition is quite likely to recur in the future.

Gastric torsion or bloat is not a condition to be under-estimated. A considerable number of large breed dogs that suffer from gastric torsion do not recover.

Pet Insurance

When you purchase a purebred dog, there is a high possibility that your dog will be subject to a number of breed-specific diseases. What's more, if you rescue a Bobtail, you may face all number of health-rated issues.

We all hope our Old English Sheepdogs will live a full and healthy life. However, when it is time for your dog to have treatment or diagnostic tests, pet insurance can help cover the medical expenses of unexpected injuries or illnesses.

For instance, when Charlie ate a pair of socks from the laundry basket, the cost came to just under $1,200. Thankfully, my brother had taken out pet insurance.

Pet insurance can cover inherited diseases such as:
- Elbow and Hip Dysplasia
- Diabetes
- Thyroid Disease
- Upper Respiratory Infections

Unidentified Issues:
- Diarrhea
- Cough
- Vomiting
- Weight Changes

Congenital Conditions:
- Heart Disease
- Cataracts
- Liver Disease
- Issues relating to the Nervous System

There are many pet insurance providers on the market today, so you will need to do your due diligence to identify the best one to suit your budget and your needs. You can do this by researching online, talking with other dog owners and your breeder, and chatting with your veterinarian.

When you have found a pet insurance plan that you think ticks all your boxes, compile a list of questions you would like to ask prospective insurers.

Photo Courtesy of Dylan Kinsella

Here are some questions you may want to ask:

- If I need to make a claim, can I choose which veterinarian I want to carry out any treatments?
- Does the plan cover examination costs?
- Do plans include preexisting medical conditions?
- What does the insurance plan include and exclude?
- Does the plan cover scheduled vet check-ups, vaccines, testing, and dental issues?
- Will the policy cover any prescription charges?
- In the event of my OES needing to be hospitalized, does the plan cover all overnight stays?
- Does the policy cover neutering or spaying?
- Does the plan cover holistic care and/or alternative therapies?
- Is there a deductibles limit?
- Are there any illness or accident caps?
- If I have to curtail travel due to my pet's illness or incapacity, will I be able to claim any personal losses?
- Can I pay for a policy via an installment plan?

How open the prospective insurer is to your questions and how well they deal with them is a good indication of the service you can expect regarding future claims.

CHAPTER 14

Nutritional And Dietary Needs

Choosing What Foods to Feed Your Adult Dog

"A quality dog food is a must. I recommend one of the ones that are suitable for all stages of life, and do not recommend puppy food. It has been show that puppy food can negatively impact bone growth in OES by making them grow too fast."

DEA FREIHEIT
SnowDowne Old English Sheepdogs

Photo Courtesy of John Dehler

Photo Courtesy of Glen & Michelle Gee

There are three conditions that can affect your Old English Sheepdog's nutrition, and they are:

> **ORTHOPEDIC DISEASE:** Large-breed dogs are prone to musculoskeletal and orthopedic disorders. These include arthritis, dysplasia, and osteochondrosis. These disorders are linked to hereditary factors, exercise, excessive growth, and nutrition. A premium quality diet with the correct balance of nutrients to help prevent muscles, joints, and bones from breaking down is advisable. Some large-breed, adult formula dog foods include glucosamine to help improve orthopedic health.

> **OBESITY:** Some breeds, like the Old English Sheepdog, tend to put on weight easily. Similar to humans, weight gain can cause health issues such as kidney disease, high blood pressure, and Type 2 diabetes. Limit treats to avoid your Bobtail packing on the pounds. You will also need to devise and adhere to an exercise regime, choose the right foods, and give them to your dog in the recommended servings and amounts. It is easy to overfeed your OES as his shaggy coat can hide extra weight, so monitor your dog's weight regularly.

> **GASTRIC TORSION/BLOAT**: This condition, discussed in the previous chapter, occurs when gases accumulate in the stomach rapidly with no means of escape. One way to avoid bloat is to avoid feeding your Bobtail

foods with a high-fat content. This can be identified as oil and fat in the first four food label ingredients.

There is no one brand of dog food that is ideal for large-breed dogs, so you will need to research which you feel is a good match for your Bobtail. The best way to do this is to ask your veterinarian to devise a lifelong nutrition plan, encompassing all stages of your Old English Sheepdog's life.

Dry Food

The majority of breeders and owners choose to serve their Bobtail dry food. It is convenient and will provide all of the nutrients your dog needs for a healthy balanced diet.

Here are some tips for choosing the right dry food for your OES.

First off, you will need only to consider feeding your OES premium range dry dog food. Good kibble must be of high quality and suit your Bobtail's nutritional breed needs.

When reading the ingredients on the back of the package, you are looking for precise and detailed compositions. Meat products should be mentioned first, with protein representing more than 25 percent of the product. The cereal percentage should be low.

Look for foods that state the kibble is cold-pressed. Cold-pressed kibble is considered to be the best dry alternative to raw food. The better the quality of the dry food, the better nourishment and greater satisfaction your Bobtail will enjoy.

One final word—unless there are added nutritional benefits, don't be tempted to break the monotony of your Bobtail's diet with alternative foods. Doing this can result in diarrhea or an upset stomach.

Photo Courtesy of Allyson Tollette

Raw Food

Uncooked and made using natural ingredients, you can either opt for ready-made or homemade raw food. Raw food is not suitable for dogs under nine months of age.

Ingredients for pet store-bought raw food are usually natural. They include human-grade raw, on-the-bone meats, vegetables, and fruits. They are ground or minced many times before being packaged and sold.

Reputable brands will display a full breakdown of ingredients; this is important to ensure your OES is getting all of his dietary needs.

Some owners who support feeding their dogs a raw diet claim that they see many positive changes in their Bobtail. These range from improved coat condition to increased energy and less smelly stools.

Homemade Raw Food

This diet is pretty much as it sounds and involves buying all the ingredients such as bone-in meat, muscle meat, and organs. You can then add your choice of vegetables (which some owners liquidize) and finally add some raw eggs, cottage cheese, or yogurt with a drop of olive oil.

Many veterinarians don't recommend homemade pet food, raw or otherwise. It is difficult to nutritionally balance food made at home, causing your Bobtail to become ill. Furthermore, raw food, and in particular meat, contains bacteria, parasites, and other pathogens that would be killed during cooking. There is also a great risk of cross-contamination. Your OES will require certain daily nutrients, so before going ahead with feeding your dog a DIY Raw diet, first, seek your veterinarian's advice.

If you decide to forge ahead with homemade dog food, adhere to these hygiene rules at all times:

- Store foods in stainless steel, glass, or metal containers as, unlike plastic, they won't develop small cracks where harmful bacteria can lurk.

- Wash your hands thoroughly before and after handling your Bobtail's food.

- Remember, animal saliva and feces can contain more bacteria when fed on raw food, so wash your hands well after touching your OES.

- Make sure your Bobtail consumes frozen foods within 24 hours of defrosting.

- Sanitize all surfaces after preparing raw food.

- Do not use a microwave to speed up the defrosting process, as this can result in an uneven thaw.

Photo Courtesy of Lynn Fine

Managing Your Dog's Weight

The recommended daily amount of premium quality dry food for your Bobtail is 2½ -4½ cups per day. A standard measuring cup is approximately 8 ounces.

An average bag of dry dog food weighs 33 pounds. A standard measuring cup is 8 ounces, which means the sack contains approximately 132 cups of food. A 30-pound bag provides 120 cups, and an 11-pound bag will give 44 cups.

The amount of food your Bobtail will need to eat each day depends on his age, size, gender, build, activity levels, and metabolism. For example, an active adult dog will need to eat more than a senior dog.

As a guide, most dogs require 25-30 calories per pound per day to maintain their weight. For instance, an adult dog weighing 60 pounds with a typical amount of exercise will need 1,500-1,800 calories per day. For dogs enjoying more than 2 hours of exercise daily, you will need to add 20 percent to these figures.

If you feed your Bobtail treats, make sure that they account for only 10 percent of his daily calorific needs and deduct the number of calories from the regular food allowance.

What Not to Feed Your OES

Foods that we, as humans, find easy to digest can be highly toxic to dogs, so don't be tempted to feed your Bobtail human treats – you may inadvertently be killing him with kindness.

Not only will certain foods upset your Old English Sheepdog's stomach, but they can also make him extremely unwell, or in a worst-case scenario, prove fatal.

Here are some foods **NOT** to feed your Bobtail:

Alcohol: Even in small amounts, alcohol, when given to dogs, can cause intoxication leading to sickness, diarrhea, and central nervous system damage.

Artificial Sweeteners: Many products are sweetened with artificial sweeteners. One such sweetener, xylitol, causes an insulin release. If your Bobtail digests a food containing this substance, he can go into a state of hypoglycemia, which is linked to blood clotting disorders and liver failure. Some brands of peanut butters contain xylitol, so always check the label before giving your dog this treat.

Photo Courtesy of Laurie Burke

Avocado: Ingesting avocado leaves, fruit, and seeds can cause vomiting and diarrhea in dogs thanks to a substance the plant contains, called persin.

Bacon and other fatty foods: These sorts of foods can have a high salt content, which can be too much for your Bobtail's digestion to handle. Eating large amounts of these foods may result in pancreatitis, which can be fatal.

Caffeine: Coffee grounds, tea bags, and diet pills all contain caffeine, which can be fatal to your dog.

Chocolate: Chocolate contains theobromine. This stimulant is toxic to canines and can result in kidney failure.

Cinnamon and cinnamon oil: Both these products can cause skin and digestion irritation in dogs.

Cooked bones: Cooked bones can splinter and perforate the gut, which can be fatal to your Bobtail.

Corn on the cob: Your Bobtail can digest corn, but the cob can create a blockage in your Bobtail's intestine and prove fatal.

Grapes and Raisins: These can cause kidney damage and liver failure when eaten by your Bobtail.

Milk and milk-based products: These can cause diarrhea, along with many other digestive issues. What's more, these products can trigger food allergies, causing your Bobtail to itch and scratch.

Nuts: Apart from being a choking hazard, nuts are high in fat and can lead to obesity. Some, like Macadamia nuts, are highly toxic and, when eaten, can affect your OES's muscles and nervous system resulting in swollen limbs, weakness, and panting.

Onion, garlic, and chives: Raw, dry, or cooked, these foods from the onion family are toxic to dogs and can cause gastrointestinal irritation and red blood cell damage.

All your Bobtail needs to stay healthy and happy is the right amount of correctly balanced food, fresh water, and good-quality recommended dog treats.

Signs your OES has ingested a toxic foodstuff

These signs will depend on the food substance or beverage your Bobtail has ingested. They will most likely include diarrhea, vomiting, shaking, coughing, sneezing, a lack of coordination, breathing difficulties, or seizure. Your dog may drink more than usual, be lacking in appetite, become sluggish, or even overly excitable. In some cases, as some reactions are not instant, your poisoned OES may not appear to be ill at all.

If you suspect your Bobtail is poisoned, first identify the source. Look for a spilled container, empty food wrappings, or torn packaging.

If your Bobtail is poisoned:

1. Remove him from the toxin. Place him in a safe space and isolate him from children and any other pets.

2. Call your veterinarian at once. If you know your OES has eaten something he shouldn't have, even if he seems perfectly well, it's better to be safe than sorry.

3. Do not attempt to induce vomiting. When ingested, some products are caustic, and so if vomited back up, it can result in severe esophageal irritation.

4. Prevent your Bobtail from grooming himself. Instead, ask your vet if you need to bathe your dog to wash away any substances.

Keeping Hydrated

A dry food diet may contain as little as five to ten percent of water and can lead to your Bobtail being thirsty. Also, foods high in sodium can cause your Bobtail to drink more.

The majority of dogs require approximately one ounce of fluids per pound of body weight per day. So an Old English Sheepdog weighing 30 pounds will need just over three cups of fresh water every day. Dogs that are very active and puppies may need more.

Monitor Your Bobtail's Water Consumption

➢ Develop a water bowl routine. Doing this will enable you to monitor your Bobtail's water consumption.

➢ Refill your Bobtail's water bowl at approximately the same time each day.

➢ Pour the water to the same level each time.

➢ Each day, make a mental note of how much water you put in the bowl and how much is left.

Dehydration

It isn't just activity levels that can affect your Old English Sheepdog's thirst, either. Hot weather can have a huge impact too, and signs that your dog is hydrated may include:

- Lethargy
- Dry tongue and gums
- Thick, rope-like saliva

If your adult OES appears mildly dehydrated but is not vomiting, give him one to two teaspoons of water every ten minutes, for three hours or so. For puppies, reduce the water dosage to one to two teaspoons.

It is essential not to give a dehydrated dog too much water at once, as this can cause vomiting.

Dehydration can become life-threatening very quickly, so if you are concerned that your Bobtail is dehydrated, seek medical care at once.

Other conditions that can lead to dehydration or excessive thirst include:

FUN FACT
Lap of Luxury

OES dogs first came to America in the late 1880s with an industrialist in Pittsburgh named William Wade. By the end of the 19th century, five of the wealthiest families in America owned Old English Sheepdogs, including the Guggenheims and Vanderbilts.

- Cancer, diarrhea, diabetes, fever, kidney disease, infection, liver disease, or Cushing' disease. Cushing's disease results when the body produces too much cortisol.

Water is vital to your Bobtail's overall health and well-being. Never forget to give your OES fresh water every day.

If you have any concerns that your Bobtail is drinking either too much or too little, don't hesitate to call your veterinarian.

CHAPTER 15
Caring for Your Senior Dog

"When an OES gets older they still want to do the things they did as a puppy, and in their mind they still think they can. Many get arthritis, just like humans do, and even though they want to desperately run and play, they just can't. There are many supplements and vitamins available that can be helpful. It's best at the first sign of them slowing down to talk with your vet and see what they recommend to best manage the arthritis. It will keep your OES more comfortable over the years."

ANNETTE P SHORE
Carolina Shores

*Photo Courtesy
of Sieglinde Schupp*

Exercising Your Senior Dog

An Old English Sheepdog is considered senior from around 4½ - 9 years of age. But just because your senior OES may have some health issues, it doesn't mean that he can't enjoy exercise. Your Bobtail may be slowing down and need more time sofa surfing, but it's still important to make sure he remains fit and healthy

Arthritis may present itself in the second half of your Bobtail's life. It can affect dogs of any size or breed. However, large dogs take part in more intensive physical exercise than small dogs, and their bodies grow quickly which makes them more likely to suffer from arthritis.

To keep your Bobtail active and help his muscles and joints, exercise should be gentle, regular, and frequent. Your OES may not be able to go on long hikes like he once did as a young dog. However, he will still benefit from stretching his legs and taking in some fresh air.

Set off on a walk and keep the route short just in case you have to head for home earlier than expected. Try to limit walks to times when the weather is not too hot, too cold, or too wet.

As your OES enters his senior years, he may start to lose his hearing or sight. When this happens, he can become anxious or confused, so it's a good idea to take him on familiar walking routes.

If during the walk, your OES is alarmed at sudden movements or unfamiliar noises, reassure him verbally and physically. Exercise at your Bobtail's pace, and don't push him to exercise for longer if he is tired. The time you spend together must be calm and enjoyable for you both.

Another great idea is to arrange supervised play dates with other senior dogs in a safe environment, such as your backyard or garden. Doing this provides an excellent opportunity to chat with someone else about any issues you face with your senior Bobtail and share some helpful hints and tips. What's more, your pets will have compatible energy levels and abilities.

Always check with your veterinarian that the level of outdoor exercise your senior Bobtail is enjoying is suitable and won't cause or aggravate any health issues or problems.

Mental Stimulation

When you can't exercise your senior OES outdoors, organize some indoor exercise and puzzle sessions at home. It is perfectly possible to teach your Old English Sheepdog new tricks!

Regardless of your Bobtail's age, provided he has a good sense of smell, he will enjoy these types of games. Better still, mental stimulation is a good way to keep your dog's brain in tip-top condition.

Puzzle toys encourage interaction, which not only gives your senior OES a physical challenge, but will also keep blood flowing to the brain. They can help stave off canine cognitive dysfunction (CCD) and give dogs suffering from dementia a well-earned workout.

Read Chapter 10 for more information about the interactive brain-training toys available for your OES.

Photo Courtesy of Peggy and Mink DiCarlo

Understanding Canine Cognitive Dysfunction (CCD)

Dementia does not just affect people; it is also something that can have an impact on dogs, too.

Although dogs don't experience dementia in the same way as humans do, what they do suffer from is similar in many ways. CCD is more present in senior pets and is considered to be the canine version of dementia.

There is, unfortunately, no cure for this condition, which is associated with the buildup of certain proteins in the brain.

Ask your veterinarian about the medications available to your dog to help reduce some of the symptoms and slow down the illness's progression.

WATCH OUT!
Popularity

The Old English Sheepdog breed is on the UK-based Kennel Club's official "At Watch" list due to a decline in popularity of the breed in recent years. The list is comprised of dog breeds with between 300 -450 puppy registrations annually. In 2018 there were 384 OES puppies registered with the club, which is a decrease of 67 percent over 20 years. Since being placed on the watch list, however, the breed has seen somewhat of a resurgence in recent years.

Warning Signs of Canine Dementia:

- **Disorientation or confusion:** Your Bobtail may appear lost in familiar places, or he may even become trapped in a room or area because he has forgotten the location of the exit

- **Toilet accidents:** Your senior OES may need more toilet breaks than usual and may have accidents inside the home

- **Changes in sleeping patterns:** Your dog may sleep a lot during the day and stay awake longer at night

- **Unfamiliar behavior:** Your senior Bobtail may become depressed, withdrawn, or even forget other family pets or even humans

- **Memory loss:** Your elderly dog may not respond to learned commands

- **Change in activity levels:** A senior dog may stare into space, pace, or not be as active as they once were

- **Changes in noise levels:** A senior Bobtail may become more vocal, especially at nighttime

- **Appetite changes:** Your Old English Sheepdog may have a decrease in appetite or an increase when he forgets that he has already eaten

What You Can Do to Help

While your Bobtail can't be cured entirely, your veterinarian can prescribe medication to help alleviate some of the symptoms of dementia. The sooner your dog begins any medication or treatment, the better, as this will help get the condition under manageable control.

Here are some helpful tips:

- Make each room in your house as familiar to your OES as you are able. Try not to unnecessarily move furniture around as this can cause confusion.
- If your senior Bobtail has a toilet accident or becomes confused, keep your cool!
- Make interaction with other members of the family, two and four-legged, a positive experience.
- Use puzzle games to help stimulate your senior Bobtail's brain.
- Take the time to retrain your dog but teaching him some of the things he may have forgotten, for instance, where to go to the toilet.
- Use environmental cues by playing music in your dog's living space. Doing this will help your senior Bobtail find his way there.

*Photo Courtesy
of Merrilee Rush*

Preventing Injury

"Many OES, even without hip dysplasia, can have trouble getting up off the floor as they age. Make sure they are not on a slippery floor. If your floor is slippery, putting down a rug helps. Try and minimize the stairs the must use if possible, and also limit jumping, as in getting on the grooming table or jumping up to get in the car."

DEA FREIHEIT
SnowDowne Old English Sheepdogs

Your senior Bobtail is more susceptible to injury. Regardless of whether this is caused by arthritis, poor eyesight, or general aging, it's your responsibility to ensure your best friend remains injury-free in his twilight years.

Your veterinarian is the first port of call when it comes to noticing any behavioral changes in your OES. He will provide you with medical advice to help prevent illness or injury. However, there are also things that you can do to make sure your home is safe for your senior OES.

A Step Up: Where once your OES could easily jump up on the sofa, climb the stairs, or jump into your vehicle, he may now not be quite so nimble. Apart from being extra patient and giving him more time, you can help prevent him from slipping or falling by investing in a ramp or cube. So check out your local pet store and search online.

Bed and Bedding: Consider buying a high-sided soft bed that is draft-free and offers the support he needs. Soft bedding will help support your senior Bobtail's tired bones and joints and prevent injury.

Dog-Proofing: Prevent your senior Bobtail from falling downstairs, hurting himself on sharp corners by dog-proofing your home using dog gates. Protect your OES from sharp door edges, table legs, and corners with bubble wrap or pipe insulation. Also, block off fireplaces, swimming pools, ponds, and any areas you deem dangerous to your senior dog. Keep floors clutter-free and cover any wires and cables.

Furniture Layout: If yoursight is failing or he lacks his usual coordination skills, place larger items of furniture against the walls and not in the center of the room. You will then need to walk him around the room, on a leash, a few times daily until he is used to the new layout.

Grooming: If your OES is experiencing decreased flexibility, he will find it more challenging to keep himself clean. Revisit your usual grooming schedule, brush him more often, and pay particular attention to the hair around the rear end, which can become matted and tangled. While grooming your senior Bobtail check for any unusual lumps and bumps. Not all lumps and bumps are cancerous; however, there is an increased risk of cancer in senior

Photo Courtesy
of Ailynn Knox-Collins

dogs. If you do feel or see anything out of the ordinary it is better to be safe than sorry; get them checked out by your veterinarian.

Lighting: A nightlight will help your senior Bobtail walk around and can be a big comfort for a vision-impaired senior dog.

Slip-free Flooring: Hard, shiny floors are slippery, and this is particularly so for an older dog. To help your Bobtail keep his paws firmly on the ground, invest in a few slip-free rugs or mats in high traffic areas.

Temperature Control: Senior Bobtails are more likely to suffer from extreme temperatures, whether too hot or too cold. If temperatures outside are falling, keep your OES indoors as much as possible. The same goes for extreme heat.

One final word: don't be tempted to allow your senior Bobtail to become a couch potato. Regular gentle exercise will help keep your Bobtail's muscles and joints supple, his mind stimulated, and his weight under control.

Identifying When It's Time to Let Go

The thought of your Old English Sheepdog dying is not something that you want to dwell on.

The reality is, though, you will most likely outlive your Bobtail.

We all hope that the ones we love pass away peacefully and without pain or suffering. However, for some of us, we have to face the fact that we may have to make the heartbreaking and difficult decision to end our dog's life.

Although aging and eventual death is not something anyone can control, you can prevent your Bobtail from a life of pain and suffering.

While medicine and surgery may be able to prolong your OES's life, it doesn't necessarily always mean that it is the right or kind thing to do.

This dilemma raises the question: "How do I know when it's time?"

When deciding what is best for your OESask yourself the following 10 questions:

1. Can your Old English Sheepdog's pain be relieved by medication?

2. Will more veterinary treatment improve your Bobtail's quality of life or only extend his already painful existence?

3. Can your dog control his bodily functions? If he can't stand, urinate, or defecate on his own, his quality of life is already miserable.

4. Is your Bobtail withdrawing from family life? Some behaviorists believe that a dog knows when it's his time to die. He may isolate himself not to

slow down the pack or cause trauma to loved ones. Your OES may avoid human contact and hide away in closed-off areas.

5. Does your OES have a healthy appetite, or has he lost interest in food?

6. What color are your Bobtail's gums? If the gums aren't pink, it's a sign that he isn't getting sufficient oxygen.

7. Does your Bobtail still enjoy being around other people and dogs? Does he recognize people he knows, or is he fearful and anxious?

8. Can your OES still play games, and does he enjoy walks and outdoor exercise?

9. If your Bobtail has a terminal illness, speak to your vet and determine what to expect at the next stage, both treatment, and pain-wise.

10. Is your vet advising euthanasia? If so, ask yourself, are you putting your needs before your dog's by delaying the inevitable?

Finally, ask yourself how many of the above points you think your Bobtail needs to enjoy a happy, healthy life. Answer honestly and make your decision based on fact, not fear.

Nobody can tell you what to do. They can only advise or give you their personal or professional opinion. Remember, if your Bobtail is suffering, then he has already lost most of the joy that comes from being a dog.

You must make your decision based on your OES's physical and mental needs rather than your own feelings or those of other family members.

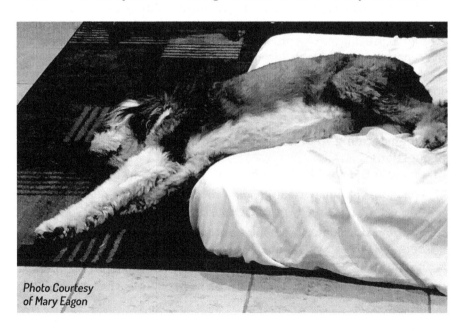

Photo Courtesy
of Mary Eagon

Euthanasia: Explained

Once you have made the difficult decision that euthanasia is the kindest option for your Bobtail, you may have questions about the procedure such as:

- Is it painful?
- Can it be carried out at home?
- May I, along with other family members, be with our pet during the process?

Having the answers to these and other questions can help you and your family come to terms with what is about to happen.

Is it painful?

Firstly, rest assured that the euthanasia procedure is not painful. Your veterinarian may first administer a sedative if your OES is scared or anxious. The sedative may sting slightly at the injection site and will sometimes have adverse side effects. These may include nausea, vomiting, salivation, mental disorientation, and more.

Talk to your vet beforehand about whether a sedative is needed. If your Bobtail is very ill, quiet, or having breathing difficulties, it may be unnecessary.

The most common euthanasia medication is a seizure medication called pentobarbital. In large doses, pentobarbital will make an animal unconscious, shutting down both the brain and heart functions within one to two minutes. It is mostly administered by IV into one leg.

As your Bobtail passes, his eyes may not close fully. He may urinate or defecate, and you may see your Bobtail twitch as he draws his final breath. The administration of a sedative makes this occurrence less likely.

All of this is very distressing, but it is a normal part of the procedure. Rest assured, your OES is in no pain.

Can it be carried out at home?

The procedure is carried out at your veterinarian's premises. For a home visit, you will need to talk with your vet and find out if it is a service he is willing to offer.

If you decide on your vet's office, then consider taking your Bobtail's bedding with you. The familiarity and smell of the blanket or pillow will help to soothe your dog.

Photo Courtesy
of Rose Weeks

May I, along with other family members, be with our Bobtail during the process?

Being present during the procedure will make the process less fearful for your Bobtail. Without your presence, the procedure will be far more traumatic.

Children may want to be with their family pet during the procedure, but keep in mind they must remain calm not to upset your dog further.

It may be a better idea to explain and discuss the procedure with them a few days before the appointment. Also, consider making a time for them to say goodbye in a less stressful environment.

The Final Farewell: Cremation versus Burial

Welcoming your OES to your home was a joyous occasion, but saying goodbye should be equally as important. Your Bobtail has been a part of your family, so recovering from his loss can be a challenge. Closure is key to moving on.

Next comes the final decision you will make for your Bobtail: whether to cremate or bury his body.

The right choice for you and your family is a personal one. It will depend on your beliefs and financial resources.

You can research what options are available in your area online or by chatting with your veterinarian.

Pet Cremation

In general, cremation is the less costly option. It needn't mean that you can't have a memorial, and private pet crematories along with the majority of vets can help with the arrangements.

There is also the option to have the remains returned to you in your vessel of choice. Doing this means you will have a lasting memorial to remember your Bobtail by.

There are several types of pet cremation options available to you. Your vet or crematory representative can help you understand what best suits your needs.

You will need to ask the crematory provider about attending the cremation.

- **Private Cremation**

This cremation is private, with only one pet being cremated in the cremation chamber at one time. This style of cremation means that you

Photo Courtesy
of Tori Theobalt

will only receive back your own dog's remains. It is the most expensive option.

- **Semi-Private Cremation**

  Some crematories may offer the option for your pet to be cremated along with others, but in a space that is portioned. While they will do their best to keep your Bobtail's ashes separate from others, it cannot be guaranteed.

- **Group or Communal Cremation**

  Here, the bodies of multiple pets are cremated in the chamber. Ashes are not returned to pet owners. Instead, they are disposed of by the facility. It is the least costly option.

Home Burial

The next option available to you is pet burial, either at home or in a pet cemetery.

Many dog owners prefer to bury their pets at home. It avoids the costs of a service and means you can plan a personal and private ceremony. It also has the added advantage that you can tend and visit your Bobtail's grave as often as you wish.

You do need to consider a few things, though, before going ahead with this type of burial.

Firstly, home-burial regulations for pets differ by municipality and state. Several factors come into play here, such as how the animal died, soil type, and water table depth.

You will need to ensure that the chosen site complies with zoning needs, property lines, and utility easements. There may also be deed restrictions relating to your neighborhood. Check also that home burial is available to rental tenants as well as homeowners. It's essential to contact the relevant county or city councils to check if your OES's home burial is legal.

If you can proceed, you will need to bury your Bobtail deep enough to prevent other animals from disturbing the grave. Should you decide to move house, it may not be possible to take your Bobtail's remains with you.

Pet Cemetery

If home burial is not an option, then a pet cemetery may be a suitable alternative. These provide a sacred and comforting place to visit your Bobtail's remains.

Pet cemeteries often offer pet burial and cremation services. These include facilities for purchasing a plot, casket, and grave, as well as holding memorial services.

Some cemeteries will help transport your Bobtail from your home or vet's office to their premises. They may offer catering services too.

Costs will vary depending on your choices and preferred level of personalization.

Veterinary Disposal

Another option available to you is veterinary disposal of your Bobtail's remains. This choice, while convenient, can make saying goodbye seem impersonal and abrupt. For some owners, it has the negative effect of delaying the healing process.

Coping with Loss

Coping with the loss of your Bobtail is a personal experience. While some owners are angry, others feel guilt. The one thing they all share, though, is a feeling of sadness.

Grief may overwhelm, come in waves, or even be delayed. Sometimes, a sight, sound, or smell can trigger memories that are as painful as they once were joyful.

It is perfectly normal to mourn the loss of a family pet, and there are ways of coping with grief.

Own your grief. In other words, don't allow others to tell you how you should feel. If you want to cry, then cry. If you want to slam the door and be angry, go ahead. Let those negative emotions out. If you have children, let them see your grief and allow them to express their sadness also.

Talk with other pet owners. If some friends and family don't understand your level of grief, talk to other dog owners who may have once experienced what you are now going through. A helpful way to do this is by researching online pet loss support groups.

Maintain a routine. If you have other pets, keep to their daily feeding, walking, and playing routines. They will be a great comfort to you, and remember, they may be feeling confused and upset by the absence of the family OES, too.

Eat, sleep, and exercise. Don't neglect your own physical and mental well-being. Spend time with the ones you love, eat healthily, get lots of sleep, and exercise regularly to boost your mood.

Celebrate your Bobtail's life. Consider planting a tree, making a photo album, or creating a legacy to celebrate your Bobtail's life. Remembering the good times you both shared as it will help you to move on. If you have children in your family, get them involved. It's an excellent way to help them deal with their loss too.

When Charlie passed on, my brother got his immediate family involved in making a memory box. He put Charlie's favorite toy, his dog tag, and a few photographs in the box. The box was kept in a safe place for a little while until the entire family felt ready to revisit the memories.

Donate. Honor your OES by volunteering at a local shelter for unwanted dogs. If you aren't ready to do hands-on help, maybe sponsor a dog, or make a donation in your Old English Sheepdog's name.

Avoid replacing your pet too soon. In time, buying another Bobtail puppy or adult may become the best option. Don't rush, though, to replace your deceased dog before the grieving process is complete. It can lead to feelings of disloyalty, especially in younger family members.

If the loss of your Old English Sheepdog is interfering long term with your everyday life, don't be embarrassed to reach out to your doctor for help and advice.

One final word: your Bobtail may no longer be by your side, but he is forever in your heart.

Made in the USA
Middletown, DE
27 August 2021